# Don't
## WAIT UNTIL Sunday!

*Devotional for Women*

Anointed Press
PUBLISHERS

Cheltenham, MD
www.anointedpresspublishers.com

# Don't
## WAIT
## UNTIL
### Sunday!

*Devotional for Women*

by: Akisha Sharon Greene

# DON'T WAIT UNTIL SUNDAY

©2012 | Akisha Sharon Greene

ISBN 13 -  978-0-9846263-9-7
ISBN 10 -  0-9846263-9-5

**To purchase additional books:**
www.anointedpresspublishers.com
www.amazon.com
*also available on Kindle*


**Cover Design:**
And How! Creative, LLC
www.andhowcreative.com
copyright © 2012


**Published by:**
Anointed Press Publishers
*(a subsidiary of Anointed Press Graphics, Inc.)*
11191 Crain Highway
Cheltenham, MD 20623
301-782-2285

# DEDICATION

Since 1970, the United States of America has recognized February as Black History Month, a time when we celebrate and commemorate the accomplishments of African Americans in America. We are very proud of and familiar with pioneers such as Rev. Dr. Martin Luther King Jr., Rosa Parks, Mary McLeod Bethune, Harriet Tubman, Jarena Lee and President Barack Obama.

I want to suggest to you today that there are countless African-American men and women, whose names will never grace the page of a history book. However, their sacrifices, hard work and dedication are just as relentless in shaping and knitting the fabric of our communities and world.

Today I stand on your shoulders and say, "Thank You."

This book is dedicated to my heroes and sheroes that have all gone from labor to reward: my pre-Kindergarten teacher and mother Sharon Deborah Greene, we only spent 27 years together, but your love and lessons have shaped my heart and being. I am honored to bear your name and legacy. I miss you so. Also, my amazing grandmothers, Norris A. Brown and Rosie P. Greene; my dear aunt, Irva Deedee Greene; my one-of-a-kind grandfather, Joe Greene; and Rev. Eliza Hammond, the first woman I saw preach the gospel of Jesus Christ with unapologetic power and authority.

# ACKNOWLEDGMENTS

I can truly say without hesitation or reservation that all I have ever needed God has provided.

God, I can't box you in; you are my Jehovah Everything! I am so glad that you are still calling and using ordinary people like me to walk on water. I am completely humbled by your love, kindness and grace toward me day after day.

Special shout out to the CEO of Team Greene, my dad, Cornelius "Big Top" Greene; my siblings, Abdul, Amar, Akeem and Alea Greene; my sisters, Arnita, Gabrielle, Danita, Shante, SeBrina, Natika, Arniece, Sylvia, Rhonda, Andrea, Chanel, LaWanza, Robrette, Nichele and Ranyne; my favorite little people in the whole world, that call me Auntie Shiesha, Aaryn, Amonte, Myla Sharon, Ahmad and Asya; my beautiful goddaughters, Briana and Stephanie; my grandfather Bertram Brown, Sr., my aunties, uncles, cousins and friends; my big sister and accountabilty coach, Tobeka G. Green; my spiritual godmother, Claudette Brown and all the amazing women of First Friday's; and my new best friend, Troy Jefferson.

Your love, encouragement and prayers have been a covering for me. I am who I am...because of you.

# INTRODUCTION

November 22, 2003, was the day my life changed forever. After having dinner with my girlfriend Chanel, my mother called my cell phone. She explained that my baby sister Alea was home from college for the weekend, and she wanted me to talk to her because she wasn't adjusting well.

"Ma, I am tired," I replied. "I will see Alea tomorrow." Someway, somehow I took the exit and ended up at my parent's house. It's funny because I realized later, when I walked in the house, my mother was washing dishes, looking out the window and never turned around to make eye contact with me. I spoke, kissed the back of her neck, and walked up the steps. When I entered the bedroom, Alea was on the phone, so I laid across my childhood twin bed and dozed off. I can still remember the chill that went up my arm at 2:10 am when my father threw opened the door and yelled "something is wrong." I sat straight up in the bed and then followed him down the steps in haste.

Nothing in Sunday school, nothing in all of my education had pre-pared me for what I was walking into. My mother was stretched out on the floor lifeless. Emergency mode kicked in. I thought she must have fallen and hit her head. I told Alea to call 911. I touched her lips, and they were cold. I didn't want to freak them out, so I told a crying Alea that she was ok, and I began administering CPR. For the next five minutes, which seemed like an eternity, I gave my mother mouth-to-mouth and chest compressions. My best efforts had failed. Tears streamed down my face as I listened to the air come back out of her mouth. Panic filled the room, and my heart sank.

This is not happening! This is a mistake! I must be dreaming! I am just 27, too young to lose my mother. Thoughts started racing through my mind. She can't leave me! What are we going to do without her! Who's going to cook Thanksgiving dinner! Whose shoulders will I cry on now! I'm not married yet! I haven't had kids yet. My worst fear came to past when the EMT arrived five minutes later and pronounced my 51-year-old mother, Sharon Deborah Greene, dead. Cause of death: heart attack.

There are no words in the human vocabulary to adequately describe the pain I felt.

There are no words to describe the void I felt. There are no words to describe my broken heart.

If I had a dollar for every tear I cried, I would already be a billion-aire.

Listening to my dad and brothers cry, made my knees numb. My family was completely devastated and our lost seemed inconsol- · able. The days and weeks following her death seemed unbear-able. I would literally lie in her closet, so I could smell her clothing. I would spray her perfume to smell her fragrance. I would call her cell phone to hear her voice. There was no remedy to fix this. There were no pills to take away the pain. There was no eraser to wipe it away. There was no ointment to lather on my broken heart.

There was no hallmark card to address my anguish. My tears literally became my petition, and everybody was leaning on me for strength! I was sick with grief and silently angry with God. I was on life support, barely breathing and functioning, and nobody knew. I lost my taste for food and my appetite for life. I took a three-month sabbatical from my job because my grief had men-tally paralyzed me. Mornings were the toughest for me because

I could not stand the notion of facing a new day without my mother. I would literally crawl out of bed in the mornings and lay on the floor until I could find the strength to face the day. Little did I know that God was using that floor as an operating table for my broken heart. Little did I know that at one of the lowest points in my life God used the floor as my launching pad. It was at that point that I realized: it is impossible to know what you're made of until your broken into pieces and the potter, God Almighty, has to put you back together again.

It was on that floor that I realized God had begun renewing my mind.

It was on that floor that I realized that I had a form of religion but not a sincere relationship with God.

It was on that floor that I realized that God was giving me 100 percent, but I was giving him only 10 percent … on a good day.

It was on that floor that I realized that God loved me and cared about what I was going through.

It was on that floor that I realized that God's strength stands up in our weakest times.

It was on that floor that I found rest in the Shadow of the Almighty.

It was on that floor that I found God to be a comforter.

It was on that floor that God gave me understanding for what I did not understand.

It was on that floor that I learned that I could trust God's heart even when I didn't understand His hands.

It was on that floor that I realized: There is a time and season for every activity under heaven ... a time to be born and a time to die. It was on that floor that I started writing sermons and preaching to myself!

It was on that floor that God's Word became a lamp unto my feet and a light to my pathway.

It was on that floor that I realized that I needed more and more of God and just Sundays wouldn't do.

It was on that floor that God literally turned my mourning into dancing.

It was on that floor that I got it in my spirit that God came and died, so that we can have an abundant life.

Now let me ask you:

What's got you on the floor?

Who has you on the floor?

How long have you been on the floor?

Are you ready to get up?

Maybe your past has you down.  Maybe it's your childhood. Maybe it's your health.  Maybe it's a family matter. Maybe it's a medical diagnosis! Maybe it's your struggle! Maybe your marriage is on life support. Maybe you are tired of being single! Maybe you are tired of being broke! Maybe you are tired of being broken!

Maybe you are unemployed! Maybe you are underemployed.

Maybe you are grieving. Maybe you are frustrated and disappointed. Maybe your best efforts have failed.

I want to suggest to you today that you don't have to wait until Sunday to reach God.

God wants to pick you up today right in the midst of what you are facing!

Life is full of ups and downs! Storms come and storms go!

It's okay to fall down, but you do not have a permission slip to stay down!

God loves you!

God cares about you!

God cares about what concerns you!

God cares about what is bankrupting your joy!

God doesn't want you going through the motions; God wants you to enjoy your LIFE!

God wants a relationship with you everyday!

You have God's ear everyday!

You have God's undivided attention everyday!

There is no grace period. There are no blackout dates! There are no restrictions or conditions!

Your benefit package extends seven days a week, 24 hours a day.

Your benefit package extends from city to city and coast to coast.

Your benefit package covers you when you are asleep and awake.

Your benefit package covers you on sunny days, rainy days, cloudy days, and don't-feel-like-being-bothered days.

So I beseech you, my sisters:

Don't give up!

Don't give in!

Don't throw in the towel!

If you have a problem you can't solve

If you have a habit you can't stop

If you have bills you can't pay

If you have a disease you can't heal

If you have trouble in your mind

If you have grief you can't comfort

If you have a past you can't erase

If you have a dream you can't finance

If you have an issue that's keeping you up at night

If you have some tears that you can't dry

If you have some deadlines that you can't meet

If you have some people that you can't please
... DON'T WAIT UNTIL SUNDAY!

God wants to give you the strategy TODAY!

DON'T WAIT UNTIL SUNDAY!
God wants you living your best life today!

DON'T WAIT UNTIL SUNDAY!
God wants to give you victory today!

DON'T WAIT UNTIL SUNDAY!
God wants to give you power today!

DON'T WAIT UNTIL SUNDAY!
God wants to strengthen you today!

DON'T WAIT UNTIL SUNDAY!
God wants to deliver you today!

DON'T WAIT UNTIL SUNDAY!
God wants to heal you today!

DON'T WAIT UNTIL SUNDAY!
God wants to comfort you today!

DON'T WAIT UNTIL SUNDAY!
God wants to promote you today!

# It's time to bounce back, and you DON'T have to WAIT UNTIL SUNDAY!

When I call your name, please grab your belongings and come forward:

Fear

Anxiety

Grief

Worry

Disappointment

Frustration

Doubt

Disease

Low Self-Esteem

Hopelessness

Past

Addiction

Jealousy

# The Tribe has spoken! You have to leave.

# From my Heart to Yours

You have the ear of God today. There are no blackout dates, restrictions or bad service areas.

Whether you are on the East or West Coast, sitting in traffic, waiting in the doctor's office, sitting behind your desk, or tossing and turning with worry and stress. Be not dismayed. God is not just willing, but God is also able to bear your burdens and encourage your heart today. No matter what you are facing today. No matter what odds are stacked against you.

Don't wait until tomorrow. Your devotion and faith are going to destroy every yolk and capture God's undivided attention today.

**Don't wait until Sunday!**
A Devotional for Women
Akisha Sharon Greene

# TABLE OF CONTENTS

HAPPY NEW YEAR - I AM GOING TO BE THE BIGGEST LOSER | 21

I'M FOLLOWING DIRECTIONS, THIS YEAR | 25

DON'T COUNT ME OUT THIS YEAR | 29

DON'T LEAVE HOME WITHOUT YOUR PERMISSION SLIP | 32

I NEED HELP | 37

I NEED A MIRACLE | 41

CAN YOU HEAR ME NOW? | 44

TAKE ME TO THE KING | 47

WHATEVER YOU DO, DON'T LOSE YOUR PRAISE | 50

I'VE GOT TO START USING WHAT I GOT LEFT | 53

I AM BOUNCING BACK | 57

I'M MOVING FORWARD | 60

STOP TALKING SO MUCH | 64

PUT YOUR HANDS UP | 69

I OWE GOD THIS | 72

THE ART OF WAR | 75

I AM GETTING THROUGH THE REST OF THIS YEAR | 78

I WILL RECOVER FROM THIS | 82

I Know Who Did It | 84

Greatness Attracts Trouble | 88

You Won't Break | 91

That's all I needed to know | 94

Stop going out of the house half dressed | 97

It's crunch time | 102

Laughing at my Pain | 104

Who told you that? | 107

Who's Spotting You? | 111

I'm Finishing Strong | 114

Don't get Amnesia | 117

You will see it, before I share it | 119

Hold on help is on the way | 122

A few rules for the Birthday Party | 125

Next Year - I am going a different way! | 129

# Happy New Year
# I am Going to be the Biggest Loser

"Therefore, since we are surrounded by such a huge crowd of witnesses to the life of faith, let us strip off every weight that slows us down, especially the sin that so easily hinders our progress. And let us run with endurance the race that God has set before us." Hebrews 12:1 NIV

You would have to live under a rock to miss the anticipation and excitement that the New Year brings. I was lying in bed and watching the marathon of NBC's, The Biggest Loser! Just in case you have never seen it: men and women travel to California for 12 grueling weeks of competition eager to change their lives one meal at a time. Pushed out of their comfort zones, the contestants have the same goal … losing weight and getting healthy.

But, they all have different excuses for why they never lost the weight before, ranging from being too busy and not knowing how to eat right, to being emotional eaters and waiting until "tomorrow" to start a weight-loss program. The contestants hit the ground running with the goal of becoming a new person and receiving the grand prize of $250,000.

The more I watched the show the more encouraged I became. So, I decided -- in order to run my race with perseverance – to take off every weight that is hindering me from being the best me.
It's inventory time!

## Inventory:

- •I am going to lose every attitude that keeps me from being the best me.
- •I am losing every habit that keeps me from being the best me.
- •I am losing excuses.
- •I am losing every weight (past mistakes, doubt, anxiety, and un-belief).
- •I am losing every stronghold.
- •I am losing the DVD of my past.
- •I am losing draining people.
- •I m losing negative thinking.
- •I am losing unfruitful conversations.
- •I am losing worry.
- •I am losing fear.
- •I am losing frustration.
- •I am losing low self-esteem.
- •I am losing complaining.
- •I am losing limits.
- •I am losing boundaries.
- •I am losing unbelief.

If you are going from good to great this year, you've got to start this year taking inventory. What do you need to lose? Who you need to lose so that you can gain?  Because what you need to gain this year is totally contingent upon what you are willing to lose.  And, you will never need another diet once you stop carrying so much weight.  In all your resolutions, resolve to be "the biggest loser" this year.

**Let us pray.**
*Acts 17:28 declares God:  it is in you that we live, move, breathe and having our being.  As the deer that pants for the water, God I come panting after you.  God, before I ask you for anything, I've got to thank you for absolutely everything.  All that I have and all that I have ever needed, God your hand has provided.*

*Thank you for how you brought me through. Thank you today for revelation. Thank you today for confirmation.  Thank you today for affirmation.  You are truly the best thing that ever happened to me.  Please don't stop until you have finished what you started in me.  As I sit at the intersection of who I was and who you have called me to be, I want you to know that I am desperate for you like never before.*

*Illuminate my strengths and identify anything or anyone that is weighing me down.  I come today giving you every sin, every weight, every pain and every problem.*

*Thank you for allowing me to see the New Year.  Thank you for new directions, new strategies, new tactics, new strengths, new ideas, new favor, new mercy, new attitudes, new habits, new friends, new mentors, new joy, new peace, new provision, new relationships, and new ventures.  Whatever you do within the next 365 days, please God don't do it without me.  In the undisputed, undefeated name of Jesus Christ I do pray.  Amen*

# New Year ~ Self Assessment

What do you need to lose this year?

_____

_____

_____

_____

_____

Who you need to lose so that you can gain?

_____

_____

_____

_____

What's your strategy to achieve your goals?

_____

_____

_____

_____

_____

# I'm Following Directions This Year!

"On the third day a wedding took place at Cana in Galilee. Jesus' mother was there, and Jesus and his disciples had also been invited to the wedding.  When the wine was gone, Jesus' mother said to him, They have no more wine.  Woman, why do you involve me?  Jesus replied.  "My hour has not yet come." His mother said to the servants, Do whatever he tells you. Nearby stood six stone water jars, the kind used by the Jews for ceremonial washing, each holding from twenty to thirty gallons.  Jesus said to the servants Fill the jars with water; so they filled them to the brim.  Then he told them, Now draw some out and take it to the master of the banquet."  They did so.  John 2:2-9 NIV

On any given day, you may pull up beside me at an intersection or a traffic light and think I am talking on my phone.  But in actuality, I am talking to my car.  Even though I have lived in the District of Columbia area my entire life, my sense of direction is simply pitiful.  So, I have this navigation system in my car that I rely on daily to get me from point A to point B.  All I have to do is type in my destination, and it will tell me how many miles away that location is.

The problem with the system is sometimes it takes me out of the way. It may take me through every light and every stop sign, or it may tell me to make a U-turn when I don't want to. Then there are times when after it tells me what to do, it just gets quiet. So sometimes, in haste or even in my own frustration, I deviate from the directions and go my own way. If it tells me to go right, then I go left. If it tells me to keep straight, then I turn. If it tells me to take a certain exit, then I don't. Isn't that just like life?

•Sometimes God shows you your destination, but He takes you the scenic route to get there.
•Sometimes God shows you your promise, and then He has you waiting at a stop sign.
•Sometimes God shows you your victory, and then He tells you to make a U-turn.
•Sometimes God lets you see your destination, and then He makes you take a detour.
•Sometimes God tells you to keep straight, and then He gets quiet.

If you are going to go from good to great this year, you have got to follow directions because that's the necessary course to reach your destination. You don't have to agree with them. You don't have to understand them. And, they don't even have to make sense.

It may look as though God is taking you off course. It may look as though God is taking you the long way. It may look as though you are lost. It may be a little uncomfortable. But even when you can't trace God's navigation system, all you can do is buckle up and trust Him. There are some things that God wants you to see and learn along journey.

So, if you are going to go from good to great do whatever God tells you to do. If He tells you to go, then go. If He tells you to stay, then stay.  If He tells you to give, then give.  If He tells you to listen, then stop talking.  If He tells you to fight, then fight.  If He tells you to save, then stop spending. If He tells you to apply, then apply. If He tells you to join a gym, then join.  If He tells you to pray at three a.m., then pray.  If He tells you to fast, then fast.

This text teaches us so many things, but the thing that stands out most is:  our miracle requires our participation.  The people didn't deviate from what Jesus told them to do. And because they followed his directions, He was able to move quickly in performing the miracle.  Stop waiting for everything to line up and make sense.  Stop waiting for people to endorse your route because this year your faith is going to defy logic.  It doesn't matter what kind of car you drive; just be sure God is in the driver seat, and you are doing what He tells you to do.  There is nothing worse than a back-seat driver.  God knows your destination. Rest on the fact that He knows the route that is best for you, and He knows when you are scheduled to arrive.

Don't just sit there.  Your miracle this year is contingent upon how well you follow directions.  What is God telling you to do?  Get out of your own way. Stop making excuses, and get moving. This year you are going from good to great!

**Let us pray.**
*God, it is in you that we live, move breathe, and have our being! Without you I am like a fish without water.  I am like a kite without wind.  God, before I ask you for anything, I've got to thank you for absolutely everything.  Thank you today for revelation.  Thank you today for confirmation.  Thank you today for affirmation. Thank you for recalculating my position.  Thank you for recalculating my condition.  You are truly the best thing that ever happened to me, so I will go wherever you want me to go and do whatever you want me to do.  Bind sickness and arrest lack.  Touch and strengthen my relationships.*

*Illuminate my directions, objectives and goals for this year. Send an Amber Alert for my lost joy. I come today giving you every weight, every pain, every problem, every issue and concern.*
*I thank you for allowing me to see this day and this year. Thank you for new directions, new strategies, new tactics, new strength, new ideas, new favor, new mercy, new attitude, new habits, new friends, new mentors, new joy, new peace, new provisions and new ventures. In Jesus' name we pray. Amen*

# Don't Count Me Out This Year

"You, dear children, are from God and have overcome them, because the one who is in you is greater than the one who is in the world." 1 John 4:4 NIV

There are very few people on the world stage that truly intrigue me. However, every since I was a little girl, I have been completely mesmerized by Oprah Winfrey. To me she is a true testament of determination, desire, drive, and old fashioned hard work. And whether or not you like her, you have to respect the fact that she has single-handedly built an empire around her very own name. From Indonesia to Pakistan, from South Africa to South America, women and men, boys and girls, everyone knows the name Oprah Winfrey. And, she has traveled a long way from Kosciusko, Mississippi, to become a regular member on the Forbes' list of wealthy. With no formal experience or training, Oprah's talk show united Americans one living room at a time. Her ratings beat out her predecessors Phil Donohue, Sally Jesse Raphael, Ricki Lake, and Geraldo Rivera. She ended her talk show after 25 years to start her "OWN" television network.

After experiencing epic success with her talk show, fans and critics alike sat on the edge of their seats in anticipation of the network's success. Unfortunately, its beginnings were slow and difficult.

Even with programming that has included fan favorites like Dr. Phil and Suze Orman, the network has not amassed the success of her show.

"How disappointed Oprah must be," I thought to myself. That was until I saw an interview with her. When asked about the failing network, Oprah replied, "Yes, I wish I would have done some things different with the launching of the OWN Network, but don't count me out just yet. I still believe in the power that works in me."

Wow! She said a lot in just a few words. I believe Oprah's public challenges with her network can teach us how to deal with our private challenges. She also shows us that even the best intentions and plans aren't exempt from life's challenges. Thus, it is essential you deal with and respond to your challenges and difficulties by standing on and relying upon the power of God that lives inside of you.

If you are facing an ailing situation or circumstance in the New Year, I want to encourage you. It's just the first quarter of the game. Get your head back in it. Don't get weary. I know you didn't see it coming, but don't abort your strategy. Start the year off by tapping into the power that is working inside of you. Get an Oprah spirit. Gather all your bills, your disappointments, your frustrations, and your critics. Clear your throat; throw your head back, and tell them, "Don't count me out just yet! I still believe in the power that's working within me!"

You can't, but God can. If God can turn water into wine, He can turn your mess into a miracle.

If He can make the sun and moon rise and fall, then He can handle you and your issues. He's greater than your biggest mistake, greater than your biggest disappointment, greater than your biggest fear, and greater than your weaknesses. His greatness is absolute. His power is undisputed. His understanding is beyond human comprehension. Know that before this year is over, there will be a performance of everything in your life that He has deposited. Don't count yourself out. God is great, and He's still making ordinary people extraordinary.

**Let us pray.**
*As David declared in the 121st Psalm, "I lift up my eyes to the mountains from where my help comes. It comes from the Lord the Maker of heaven and earth." Like a deer pants for water, like the desert needs rain, like the morning needs sunlight, like the ocean needs the stream, God I come longing for you. I come desperate for you. All that I have needed, God it was your hand that provided.*

*Deliver the bound. Lift depressed heads. Comfort mourning hearts. Eradicate financial woes. Open doors. Revive dead relationships. Rebuke all infirmities, afflictions, inflammation, sickness, and disease in your people. Illuminate my dreams. Strengthen my determination. I thank you for the power that you have given me to decree and declare your will for my life. Thank you for not counting me out. I love you Jesus! Amen.*

# Don't Leave Home Without Your Permission Slip

"They sailed to the region of the Gerasenes, which is across the lake from Galilee.  When Jesus stepped ashore, he was met by a demon-possessed man from the town.  For a long time this man had not worn clothes or lived in a house, but had lived in the tombs.  When he saw Jesus, he cried out and fell at his feet, shouting at the top of his voice, What do you want with me, Jesus, Son of the Most High God? I beg you, don't torture me!  For Jesus had commanded the evil spirit to come out of the man. Many times it had seized him, and though he was chained hand and foot and kept under guard, he had broken his chains and had been driven by the demon into solitary places.  Jesus asked him, "What is your name? Legion, he replied, because many demons had gone into him.  And they begged him repeatedly not to order them to go into the Abyss. A large herd of pigs was feeding there on the hillside. The demons begged Jesus to let them go into them, and he gave them permission.  When the demons came out of the man, they went into the pigs, and the herd rushed down the steep bank into the lake and was drowned."  St. Luke 8:26-33 NIV

The older I get the more I realize that there are some lessons in life that you will never forget, like the time in fifth grade when my class was going to see Willy Wonka and the Chocolate Factory at the E Street Cinema. I was so excited. I got home that afternoon, laid out my uniform, and did my homework early so I could go to bed early in anticipation of the next day.

I even did some extra chores around the house the weekend before so I could earn some money for popcorn and candy. The next day I got up early; my mother had already fixed my favorite lunch: a peanut butter and jelly sandwich cut in four squares on soft Wonder Bread, a bag of potato chips and a Sip Up.

My job in the mornings was to clear the counter from breakfast, help my mother get everyone's coat on, and get them in the car. I made sure I was on my job early, so we wouldn't be late.

I arrived to school early, kissed my mother goodbye, told my brothers and sister to have a good day, and ran to my classroom. Once in the room, I hung up my coat and took my seat. I was ready for my trip to the movies with my friends. After our morning prayer and the Pledge of Allegiance, Sister Theresa pulled her list out. She said, "I will be calling the names of everyone with a signed permission slip to get in line so that we can start boarding the bus."

I zipped up my coat, put my gloves on, and grabbed my lunch bag. Then I noticed that Sister Theresa was done calling names. Todd, Dominique, and I were still sitting in our seats.

My heart skipped a beat. I knew why they were still sitting there, but it made no sense why I was still sitting there. Running to her desk with tears streaming down my cheeks I said, "Sister Theresa there must be a big mistake; there must be some type of conspiracy! I gave you my permission slip two weeks ago." Sister Theresa said,

"Honey, I believe you, but I can't find it. It's not here." "How did this happen?" I thought. I was devastated.

I was unable to join my classmates for the field trip because my teacher didn't have permission to take me off the school's premises. She didn't have my parents' consent for me to leave the school, and she didn't have authorization for me to get on the bus. Tell your circumstances: "Not today, you don't have my Father's permission to ruin my day." Tell your coworkers: "Access denied. You don't have my Daddy's permission to get on my nerves today." Tell your doctor's report: "You don't have permission to invade my body." Tell fear and worry: "You don't have permission to paralyze my faith." Tell struggle: "You don't have permission to occupy my future."

I love this text because it reminds us that the earth belongs to the Lord. That means everything and everyone is under the subjection of our God. In other words, everything and everybody, every force, every authority, every demon here and in hell, every storm is under the power, rule and authority of God. The demons could not just do what they wanted to do or go where they wanted to go. They had to ask Jesus for permission before making a move. That's good news because that means nothing just happens to me.

It might catch me by surprise, but it doesn't catch God by surprise. Even the winds and waves are under the subjection of God. The birds and trees, Democrats and Republicans, my friends and enemies, are all under the subjection of God. Everything concerning me and surrounding me is under the subjection of God. So I believe God, and I will live my life unapologetically.

I have permission to be who He has called me to be. I have permission to have what He said I can have. I have permission to live more abundantly. I have authorization to be blessed in the city and in the field. I have permission to be allergic to lack. I have

God's permission to live in overflow. I have God's consent to have joy.

If you want to get through the rest of this year, make sure you know that you have a divine permission slip, signed by the author and finisher of our faith. It's the Word of God. Flash it. Use it. Quote it. Stand on it. Get it in your heart. Get it on your mind. Get it in your spirit.

**Let us pray.**
*Walter Hawkins wrote, "Tragedy is common place, all kind of diseases, people are slipping away, the economy is down people can't get enough pay, as for me, all I can say is, 'Thank You Lord for all you've done for me!'"*

*Thank you for keeping me, loving me, and making a way for me. Thank you for providing for me. God you are the lifter of my head, and the provider of all my needs. I thank you that when I didn't have society's permission, I had yours ... favor! Don't let me leave this page still frustrated! Don't let me leave this page still disappointed. God arrest sickness, disease, suicide, depression and worry.*

*You are great. You are awesome. Send me a new portion of strength. Send me a fresh outpouring of your glory. Send me a new portion of favor. Send me a new portion of hope. I deem it already done in the undisputed, undefeated name of Jesus. Amen.*

# Closing Thoughts

Aren't you glad that you have God's permission slip?  You can't give it away. You can't throw in the towel or lose your mind.  You can't lose this fight because you have God's permission slip to be victorious.

(Romans 8:37)

# I Need Help

"So Joshua fought the Amalekites as Moses had ordered, and Moses, Aaron and Hur went to the top of the hill. As long as Moses held up his hands, the Israelites were winning, but whenever he lowered his hands, the Amalekites were winning. When Moses' hands grew tired, they took a stone and put it under him and he sat on it. Aaron and Hur held his hands up—one on one side, one on the other—so that his hands remained steady till sunset." Exodus 17:10- 12

My parents were very big on teaching us the importance of being self sufficient. Webster's Dictionary defines self sufficiency as "the art of being able to provide for yourself, being self reliant, self sustaining, and independent."

One weekend as I prepared to move, I really began to think about what it meant to need help. While I had packed all the boxes, many of them were too heavy for me to lift. As self sufficient as I was, I still needed help. Independence is important and necessary, but there comes a time in life when we all will need help, assistance, and support from others.

That's why I love this scripture. As long as Moses held up his staff the Israelites prevailed; when he lowered it, the enemy gained the advantage. Moses was human like the rest of us. His arms became tired, and he could no longer hold them up. Aaron and Hur found a stone for him to sit on, and they stood on each side of him and held his hands. God not only gave Israel the victory that day, but He showed Moses, you and I that there are times in life when we all will need some help.

We need:
- Help fighting the good fight when our arms get tired
- Help believing when our faith is tired
- Help praying when our throat gets tired
- Help smiling when our heart gets tired
- Help praising when our feet get tired
- Help sitting down so that God can stand up
- Help believing the impossible
- Help seeing the invisible
- Help loving those who hate us

Songwriter Bill Withers said it this way, "Sometimes in our lives we all have pain. We all have sorrow, but if we are wise we know that there is always tomorrow. Lean on me." Make sure you've got someone strong because everybody sooner or later will need somebody to lean on!

**Let us pray.**
*God the Bible says you are my refuge and strength, a very present help in trouble. I thank you today for being consistent. Thank you for being reliable. Thank you for not going on vacation. Thank you for not screening my calls. Thank you for coming to my rescue. Thank you for not turning your back on me. Thank you for being sovereign. Thank you for being mighty. Thank you for being amazing.*

*Thank you for this day, a day that I have never seen before and will not see again. I don't want to beat around the bush. I need your help. Help me to keep going and not give up or give in. Help me to believe and not sink in my circumstances. Help me to stop living in the past and embrace the plans you have for me. Help me to stop wasting time. Help me to get past the pain. Help me to accept help from others. Help me to get through what I am facing. Help me to believe – in spite of it all – that what's to come is better than what has been.*

*I don't want to waste this day away. I don't want to worry this day away. I don't want to cry this day away. I really need your help to take it one day at a time. Breathe new strength into my nostrils. I need your joy and peace.*

*Dispatch new friends into my circle that will hold up my hands. Give extra credit to the friends who have held me up season after season. Thank you for grace to trust you more. Thank you for counting every tear. And, thank you that when I ask you for one thing, you always show up with everything. Amen.*

# Self Assessment

What areas of your life do you need help with?

_____

_____

_____

_____

_____

_____

_____

Are you ready to admit that you need help?

_____

_____

_____

_____

_____

_____

_____

# I Need a Miracle

"On his arrival, Jesus found that Lazarus had already been in the tomb for four days. Now Bethany was less than two miles[b] from Jerusalem, and many Jews had come to Martha and Mary to comfort them in the loss of their brother. When Martha heard that Jesus was coming, she went out to meet him, but Mary stayed at home. Lord, Martha said to Jesus, if you had been here, my brother would not have died. But I know that even now God will give you whatever you ask. Jesus said to her, Your brother will rise again. Martha answered, I know he will rise again in the resurrection at the last day. Jesus said to her, I am the resurrection and the life. The one who believes in me will live, even though they die; and whoever lives by believing in me will never die." John 11: 17– 25

After three years and the loss of her publishing rights on six out of her 10 books, Iyanla Vanzant decided to sit down and write again. She gives the public a front row seat into her private pain. Her book, Peace with Broken Pieces, chronicles in 20 chapters, 565 pages, how at 58 years old, she was still carrying around past hurts: the death of her mother, the emotional abandonment of her father, the physical abuse by her grandmother, the sexual abuse by her uncle, the loss of her marriage, the death of her oldest daughter, and the loss of her home. However, something happened. Just when the critics were about to write her off and book her for the next "Where are they Now" special, she found the power within to give God all of her broken pieces.

She gave God her grief, pain, heartbreak, disappointment, fear, and humiliation. I read the book. I watched the final interview on the OWN network. And, I still couldn't figure out how someone who had gone through so much, cried so much, lost so much, have such peace. How could she smile when she had so much to cry about? Then I ran into this scripture.

This is a familiar text, but God offered me fresh insight. Just like Iyanla – Martha had some broken pieces too. It was just the three of them, and after all they had gone through, their family circle had been broken. Lazarus had died. His obituary was already in the Washington Post. The wake and the funeral were over; his body had already been laid to rest. The folks were back at the house eating chicken and reminiscing about the good ole days. Then Jesus appears on the scene, and the Bible says, "Jesus shows up distressed, troubled, and a little upset.

Jesus was not distressed because Lazarus was dead. He was distressed because after He had fed five thousand people with two fish and five loaves of bread, they still didn't believe He was who He said He was.

That's just like us. After all the life we've lived, by now, we should have some history, a track record with God. By now you should be able to look back over your life and the things that you have been through and have some evidence. The Bible says Jesus tells them to remove the stone, but Martha responds: "It's been four days; the body is already stinking!"

This year, you've got to stop telling God how stinky your situation is, and tell him "I need a miracle." Stop telling God how stinky

42

your circumstances are, how tight your finances, and just tell him you need a miracle.

A miracle is defined by Webster's Dictionary as "a divine intervention in a natural circumstance; a divine intervention that defies the natural or scientific law." If you're going from good to great this year, it's not going to be by your might or power, but it's going to take a miracle! I don't know about you, but I need a miracle!

**Let us pray.**
*All powerful and everlasting God, our Jehovah Jireh, I don't need another degree, I need a miracle. I don't need another pair of high heels, I need a miracle. You're awesome. You're holy. You're altogether lovely. You still have the power to do the miraculous. I need you to shower down your signs and wonders. Touch closed wombs. Comfort grieving hearts. Resuscitate relationships on life support. Heal depressed and worried minds. Raise dead dreams. Ease aches and erase pains. Rebuke the enemy. Destroy every yolk and stronghold. Give me the serenity to accept the things that I cannot change. Give me the courage to change the things that I can. And, give me the priceless wisdom to know what needs to stay dead and what needs to be revived in my life. Amen*

# Can You Hear Me Now?

"The LORD said, Go out and stand on the mountain in the presence of the LORD, for the LORD is about to pass by. Then a great and powerful wind tore the mountains apart and shattered the rocks before the LORD, but the LORD was not in the wind. After the wind there was an earthquake, but the LORD was not in the earthquake. After the earthquake came a fire, but the LORD was not in the fire. And after the fire came a gentle whisper. When Elijah heard it, he pulled his cloak over his face and went out and stood at the mouth of the cave. Then a voice said to him, What are you doing here, Elijah?" I Kings 19: 11-13

In 2002, Verizon Wireless launched a brilliant advertising campaign that took the wireless market by storm. The company hired 34-year-old test man, Paul Marcarelli, a New York City native and starving artist.

Marcarelli posed one question, not super deep, but super effective. He asked, "Can you hear me now?" By posing and answering this one question, the company strengthened its profile and reduced its customer turnover by leaps and bounds. The challenge to competitors was not over pricing, plans, features, or phone models; it was over reliability.

Whether you find the question, "Can you hear me now?" annoying or amusing, at least be fair and admit it was effective. Because whether you have Verizon Wireless, AT&T, Spring, T-Mobile, Cricket or Boost Mobile, everyone wants a phone on which they can depend.

I need to know if I get a flat tire or get sick I can get a call through. I want and need to know after I have been there for you that you will be there for me. I need to know after I have prayed for you that you will pray for me. I need to know that what I tell you is between you and me. I need to know that after I have sacrificed for you that you will sacrifice for me. I need reliability.

This brings us to the heart of the matter. Elijah was in trouble. He was actually running for his life and while running he found shelter in a cave where he had a pity party. If he could sing like Smokie Norful, he would have said, "Lord if you hear me I'm calling you. Do you see; do you even care about what I'm going through."

Then suddenly God tells Elijah to go and stand on the mountain because He is about to pass by. But, if you keep reading you will notice that Elijah doesn't move until later. For the rest of this year, follow instructions. If God says move then move. If God says go then go. If God says start then start. If God says stop then stop. If God says walk away then run.

The Bible says wind, an earthquake and fire came, but God wasn't in any of it. For the rest of this year, stop looking for God to just reveal God's self in big loud ways. God can speak in a whisper. And, I believe much of what we go through in life is God trying to get us out of the cave mentality. The noises in your life have derailed not only your actions but also your attention. If you don't get quiet, you are going to miss hearing the voice of God. God is saying: "Can you hear me now. I am speaking. I am reliable, and I can be what you need." If you need God to be a parent then God will be that. If you

45

need God to be a physician then God will be that.  If you need God to be strength then God can be that too.   God is reliable.   Can you hear God now?

*Let us pray.*
*Yes, God. I hear you loud and clear.  As bees chase after the honey, without reservation or hesitation, God, I am chasing after you. It is in you that I live, breathe, move, and have my being.*

*Thank you for being dependable and reliable.  Thank you that no matter where I go, I will never lose your coverage.  Thank you for being powerful and mighty. Thank you for hearing my moans and drying my tears.  Thank you for loving me even when I wasn't lovable.  In spite of all of my uncertainties, God I am certain about you. Touch me as I pray this prayer. Search the city of my soul.  Deposit whatever I need.  Withdraw whatever is draining my life's account. Touch my family, friends and enemies.*

*God, I come today with Holy Ghost confidence that my concerns are your concerns and my cares your cares.  Thank you for healing. Thank you for employment.  Thank you for reviving my hopes and resuscitating my dreams.  Thank you for comforting my heart. And, thank you for whispering the plans, goals, and objectives you have for me for the remainder of the year.*

*I come declaring and decreeing, even in a recession, you have marvelous and mighty plans for my life. I come declaring and decreeing that I am getting up and getting out of the cave of cheap and low living.  I come declaring and decreeing that I can hear you now.  I love you.  I adore you. Thank you for giving me the ears to hear your voice. Amen.*

# Take Me to the King

"A few days later, when Jesus again entered Capernaum, the people heard that he had come home.  They gathered in such large numbers that there was no room left, not even outside the door, and he preached the word to them.  Some men came, bringing to him a paralyzed man, carried by four of them.  Since they could not get him to Jesus because of the crowd, they made an opening in the roof above Jesus by digging through it and then lowered the mat the man was lying on.  When Jesus saw their faith, he said to the paralyzed man, Son, your sins are forgiven."  Mark 2: 1- 5

Actress and powerhouse vocalist Tamela Mann is back with a new single, "Take Me to the King."  I'm not sure if you have heard it yet, but she sings, "Take me to the King, I don't have much to bring, my heart and soul is in pieces and it's my offering.  Take me to the King."

And she is not by herself.  Many feel like they are at the end of their line. It could be you.  Are you tired? Do you feel like you're out of health, out of money, out of tears, out of friends, out of sleep, and out of patience?  Do you feel like you're out of your faith?  The Bible says that when Jesus entered Capernaum the people came in droves. They gathered in such a great number that there was no room left, not even outside the door.

The thing that amazes me is: how did the people know Jesus was coming? There was no Internet, Twitter or Facebook, but the people came. Some people probably came to hear if Jesus could preach. Others probably came to see who would be there.

Regardless of their reasons, the room was beyond capacity. Then these folks show up with a problem that they could not solve. Their friend had a sickness that could not be healed.

There were questions they couldn't answer, circumstances they could not fix, and tears they couldn't dry. They had made up in their minds that they were going to get to Jesus no matter what it took. If they couldn't get in through the door, then they would climb up to the roof. They didn't care how they looked or what people thought. They were on a mission to take their friend to the King.

You can't, but God can. The doctors can't, but God can. Congress can't, but God can. The bank can't, but God can. Your family can't, but God can. For the rest of this year, stop wasting time telling your problems to people who have more problems than you. You've got to take it to the King! For the rest of this year, stop allowing your ears to become a dumping ground for people and their issues. You've got to tell them to take it to the King.

**Let us pray.**
*You are holy, oh so holy. What a privilege and an honor to worship at your throne.*

*The Bible says you know my beginning, middle and ending. Thank you for reminding me of that today; that nothing is impossible for you. You have everything I need. You are the source of my strength and strength of my life. Thank you today for canceling the plot that the enemy had for me.  Thank you today for making your grace sufficient.  Thank you today for destroying every yolk and stronghold.  Thank you today for giving me power to tread on the enemy.  Thank you for giving me the vision to see the invisible and the impossible.  Thank you for always being available and accessible.*

*Thank you for healing my mind and comforting my heart.  Thank you for not turning your ringer off and for always hearing my prayers.  Thank you for paying bills that I cannot pay!  Thank you for solving problems I can't figure out.  Thank you for loving me when I wasn't lovable.*

*So now unto you God, who is able to do immeasurably more than my mind could ask, think, dream or imagine according to your power that is working within me. To you God be the glory and the power.  In the undisputed, undefeated name of Jesus I do pray. Amen.*

# Whatever You Do, Don't Lose Your Praise

"Those who sacrifice thank offerings honor me, and to the blameless[a] I will show my salvation." Psalm 50: 23 NIV

"I will sacrifice a freewill offering to you; I will praise your name, LORD, for it is good." Psalm 54:6 NIV

"Through Jesus, therefore, let us continually offer to God a sacrifice of praise—the fruit of lips that openly profess his name." Hebrews 13:15 NIV

After leaving the doctor's office in December 2010, I made up in my mind that the New Year was going to be a lifestyle change for me. Not a New Year's resolution or a quick fix. So on January 1, 2011, I made a promise to myself and God that I was going to make exercise a part of my lifestyle. No excuses. I joined my neighborhood gym, invested in some good tennis shoes and workout clothes, got a personal trainer, and changed my diet. I can stop right here and testify. I am 30 pounds lighter, and it's been a journey. I am still learning new lessons about the art of sacrifice and discipline in the area of eating.

When you start talking about sacrifice, people get nervous because we like getting without the responsibility of giving. This attitude carries over into our relationship with people and with God. Sacrifice means:

- It's going to cost you something.
- You're making an offering.
- You're coming out of your comfort zone.
- You're surrendering to God's will and way.

Today, I come as your Holy Ghost cheerleader to say "Despite what you may have lost, hold onto your praise." You may have lost some loved ones, but don't lose your praise. You may have lost possessions, but don't lose your praise. You may have lost some of your hope, but don't lose your praise. You may have lost some sleep, but don't lose your praise. You may have lost your strength, but don't lose your praise. I know some of you have lost some hair! I know some of you have lost some joy!

Whatever you do, don't lose your "hallelujah" or your "Thank You Jesus." Don't lose your hand clapping or your foot stomping. Praise is a weapon, and it has the power to change your position and your condition.

All of us have tests, troubles, and trials. Today, I must remind you, like I have to remind myself quite often, that God has promised morning joy for our nighttime crying. And, morning has nothing to do with the time on a clock. Morning is when you look at your situation or circumstance and say, "It's a new day. I cried over yesterday, but it's a new day. I was hopeless yesterday, but it's a new day." You can't resign. You can't give up. You can't quit. You can't die.

God's invested too much in you, and He expects a return on His investment. God inhabits the praises of His people (Psalms 22:3). That means God dwells and abides in praise. I heard Bishop Frank

Gibson say it this way, "If you want to see if a Christian is alive, don't check the pulse. Check the praise." You've got to make up in your mind, that you shall live and not die.

**Let us pray.**
*I recognize that you God are worthy of all honor, praise, and worship. I ask that you release the fullness of your Holy Spirit in my mind, body, and soul today. I ask in the name of Jesus that you rebuke all infirmities, afflictions, inflammation, sickness, and disease in me, my family and friends.*

*I thank you for the power that you gave us to decree and declare, so I decree and declare that during the next 30 days I will see your miracles, signs, and wonders. I decree and declare that anybody I am connected to who is unemployed will gain meaningful employment before this month is over. I decree and declare that the issue that's been keeping me up at night is going to be resolved before the month is out. Please don't stop until you finish what you started in me. I am not Jabez, but I am calling on you, the God of Israel, "Oh that you would bless me indeed (I Chronicles 4:11). In the name of Jesus Christ. Amen.*

# I've Got to Start Using What I Got Left

According to the World Health Organization, there are 650 million people in the world with some type of disability. A disability can be physical such as deafness or blindness, or it can be something you cannot see such as autism or a mental illness.

Some people are born with a disability. In John chapter nine Jesus passed by a man who was born blind, and the disciples asked Jesus, "Who sinned, him or his parents?" And Jesus replied that no one had sinned. God's going to get the glory out of this!

Others may become disabled as a result of an accident or disease. Remember Christopher Reeves, the actor who played Superman? On the movie screen, he could fly through buildings and pick up cars, but in reality, a horse riding accident left him paralyzed from the neck down.

Or how about in Exodus, when God commissioned Moses, "to go and tell Pharaoh let my people go." And Moses said, "Lord, did you forget that I have a disability? I stutter." (Exodus 4:10).

Sometimes God will tell you do something, or give you a task that seems impractical. He may show you dreams that don't match your resources. He may show you a job you don't possess the skills to qualify. Or, He may show you a house you can't afford. It may seem like the odds are stacked against you.

That's why I love the story of Liu Wei. As I was perusing YouTube one night, I ran across China's Got Talent competition, the America's Got Talent equivalent. People from across the country come and stand in exhausting lines to showcase their talent. After weeks of fierce competition, Wei made it to the final round, bringing the audience to tears and getting a five-minute standing ovation for his rendition of James Blunt's, "You are Beautiful." Wei masterfully played the song not missing a single key. That may not mean much to you until you understand that Wei has no arms.

When I watched the documentary on him, I learned it wasn't until he lost his arms that he relearned how to use his legs and feet. It wasn't until Warren Buffett was denied entrance into Harvard that he started using his legs and feet. It wasn't until Mark Zuckerberg, founder of Facebook, felt like a social misfit that he started using his legs and feet. It wasn't until Michael Jordan was denied by his high school basketball team that he started using his legs and his feet. It wasn't until Rosa Parks had to go the back of the bus that she started using her legs and feet. What you lost wasn't intended to break you; it was intended to make you!

It always blows my mind, as I people-watch, how a disability can cause one person to give up and another one to start over. What makes one person fall down and another person get back up? What makes one person throw in the towel and another person wipe his/her head with it? What makes one person get stuck in the past and another jaywalk into the present?

Today, I don't know where you are in your journey. I don't know what debt ceilings are tapping at your head! You may not have lost a limb. You may not have lost your sight. You may not have lost your hearing. You may not have lost your hair to cancer! You may not have lost your mobility to a wheelchair!

Whether it's your job, your relationship, your fight, your smile, your sleep, your dreams, your joy, or your strength, I've come to encourage you to use what you've got left.

The story of Moses teaches us how God calls us despite our disabilities. God still called him. God still used him. God still blessed him. Therefore, stop allowing people to disqualify you because of what makes you different. Just like God chose Moses, God chooses you. Your disadvantage is going to be your advantage. In this new season, the very thing that had disabled you is going to position you for your future. For the rest of this year, do me a favor, take inventory, and start using what you've got left!

**Let us pray.**
*Father God I thank you for Jesus your Son. Thank you for giving me the strength to stop mourning over what I lost. Thank you for giving me the strength to tap into what I have left. Thank you for protecting, keeping, leading, and guiding me in the process.*

*Breathe on my family today. Breathe on my finances today. Breathe on my workplace today. Where somebody needs a job, I decree and declare employment. Where there's lack, I speak overflow. Where there is pain, I speak comfort. Where there is sickness, I speak healing. Where there are tears, I speak your peace. Where there is cancer, I speak Jesus. Where there is AIDS, I speak Jesus. Where there is diabetes, I speak Jesus.*

*Search me. Purge me, and cleanse me from any habit, any memory, any hurt, any pain, and anybody that would prevent me from using what I have left and being the best reflection of you.*

*It is in the matchless name of Jesus! Amen.*

# Self-Assessment

What have I lost this year?

_____

_____

_____

_____

Who have I lost this year?

_____

_____

_____

_____

What attributes do I have left?

_____

_____

_____

_____

# I am Bouncing Back

"David noticed that his attendants were whispering among themselves, and he realized the child was dead. Is the child dead? He asked. Yes, they replied, he is dead. Then David got up from the ground. After he had washed, put on lotions and changed his clothes, he went into the house of the LORD and worshiped. Then he went to his own house, and at his request they served him food, and he ate. His attendants asked him, Why are you acting this way? While the child was alive, you fasted and wept, but now that the child is dead, you get up and eat! He answered, While the child was still alive, I fasted and wept. I thought, Who knows? The LORD may be gracious to me and let the child live. But now that he is dead, why should I go on fasting? Can I bring him back again? I will go to him, but he will not return to me." II Samuel 12: 19-22 NIV

I have never professed to know everything. One thing I do know is that no matter how rich, how poor, how smart, how talented, whether you're white collar, blue collar, or no collar, no one is immune to the tests and trials of life. As much as we profess our differences, there is an undeniable commonality to the sufferings and pains of this life. Hard times don't discriminate; they hit us all. These sufferings don't call or RSVP; they just show up. From the pulpit to the pew, the storms of life have the unique ability to knock us all down ... physically, spiritually, emotionally, and financially.

The longer I live the more I realize it's not about how we go down, but how well we get back up from our setbacks, adversity, and frustrations. That's why I love this scripture. David experienced every parent's nightmare. Even after the tears, prayers and fasting, his son still died. The text doesn't share how old the boy was, his name or hobbies. All we know is that he died. Let's park right here.

I have never buried a child, but I have buried a mother, two grandmothers, a grandfather, my little cousin, and my aunt. So, I know how grief can knock you so low you feel like you are tasting dirt. From that I have learned that you will never know that Jesus is all you need, until you realize that Jesus is all you have. I know the Bible says, "to be absent from the body is to be present with the Lord" (II Corinthians 5:8), but grief can be so heavy that if you're not careful it will paralyze you. It can become like quick sand and slowly suffocate your joy and peace of mind.

Life had knocked David down. As I interrogated the text, I said, "David, I need to know how you got up and found the strength to go on? How did you eat when life had taken your appetite? How did you find the power to get up when God didn't honor your prayer request?"

David responded, "After I cried and cried, after I wept and rolled around the floor, I reminded myself that no matter what I go through nothing will separate me from the love of God. When I began to worship – with tears streaming down my face – I asked God to give me strength to live with what I could not change. When I stopped worrying about who was looking at me, I lost myself in worship and God renewed my strength. He gave me beauty for ashes, the oil of joy for mourning, and the garment of praise for the spirit of heaviness (Isaiah 61:3).  When you praise God, God stops what He's doing and comes and sits in the middle of your situation."

**Let us pray.**

*Dear God, I need you!  This is more than I can handle.  Please help me in this time of loss and mourning.  I am consumed with grief. Touch my heart; it's broken. Dry my tears. Help me through this pain, so that I won't lose my hope in you.  Give my mind a peace that surpasses all human understanding.  You have promised me everlasting consolation and hope through your precious grace. Please help me through this, so I can bounce back.  In Jesus Name I pray.  Amen.*

# I'm Moving Forward

"Not that I have already obtained all this, or have already arrived at my goal, but I press on to take hold of that for which Christ Jesus took hold of me. Brothers and sisters, I do not consider myself yet to have taken hold of it. But one thing I do: Forgetting what is behind and straining toward what is ahead, I press on toward the goal to win the prize for which God has called me heavenward in Christ Jesus."
Philippians 3:12-14 NIV

In the midst of a tough economy, in September 2011 over one million people paid $60 to HBO for an all access pass from the comfort of their home to watch the boxing match between Floyd Mayweather and Victor Ortiz.

Whether or not you are still debating or disputing the merits or the outcome of the fight, at the end of the fourth round, the referee declared Mayweather to be the winner and undisputed champion. I must admit that I am not a big fan of Mayweather's arrogance or flashy style, but I do respect his will, determination and his discipline to remain a winner.

Can you imagine how different your life would be if you woke up tomorrow with an unapologetic arrogance to win? Can you imagine how different your life would be if your faith was arrogant?

As I drove to church the Sunday after the fight, my thoughts were of Victor Ortiz. I watched how hard he trained. I saw how bad he wanted it. How was he able to move forward in the fight, knowing the odds were against him. He must have known people were expecting him to lose, but who enters the ring of life expecting not to win?

So what do you do when your training efforts still come up short? What do you do when suddenly without warning and often without apparent provocation you are "sucker punched" by the adversary?

What do you do when you love them and they hate you? What do you do after you've got there early and stayed late and you still don't get the promotion? What do you do after you've applied and you still can't find a job? What do you do after you've raised your kids to do right, and they don't? What do you do when it seems like the more you pray the worse they act? I am so glad you asked. I believe this scripture is clear.

You press past your disappointments. Press past your frustrations. Press past your past mistakes. Press past your pain. Press past your tears. Press past your feelings. Press past your diagnosis. Press past our fears. And, press past your worries. Your recovery is in your pressing. Your breakthrough is in your pressing. Your deliverance is in your pressing, and your destiny is in your pressing.

You may get knocked down, but you can't stay down. You may get bruised, but you will heal. Whatever you do, keep moving. Whatever you do keep pushing toward what God said. If you want to make it through this year and win, it's got to be intentional. It's not going to happen by accident or osmosis.

You've got to press like your future depends on it. Stop turning around. Stop looking around. Stop waiting for others to endorse your press.  Stop dwelling on past disappointments and frustrations.  Stop playing the DVD of your losses.  Stop letting your critics and enemies distract you.  Declare yourself a winner even when it seems like you're losing because it's all working together for your good.

God has a plan with you in mind. He desires that  you be fruitful and multiply.  He knows your beginning and ending.  Don't be dismayed.  It's not just your time to win.  It's your turn to win.

Let the world have its trinkets, titles, and belts,  but don't lose your arrogance to win.  Your losses can't compare to what you're going to gain.  You may not have all of the answers, but purpose in yourself to move forward even if you have to crawl.

# Self-Assessment

What has knocked you down in the ring of life?

_____

_____

_____

_____

_____

_____

Write a "Moving Forward" Prayer to God:

_____

_____

_____

_____

_____

_____

_____

_____

_____

# Stop Talking So Much

"A wise man will hear and increase in learning, and a man of understanding will acquire wise counsel." Proverbs 1:5 NIV

"He who has an ear, let him hear what the Spirit says to the churches." Rev. 3:22 NIV

"While he was speaking, a bright cloud enveloped them, and a voice from the cloud said, This is my Son, whom I love; with him and well pleased. Listen to him!" Matt 17:5 NIV

I have not physically birthed a child ... yet. However, I can clearly remember the joy of hearing my nieces' and nephews' first words. It was such a profound moment in the lives of their parents and our entire family. The joy of hearing the first "dada" or "mama" is priceless.

In one of its reports, the American Academy of Pediatrics suggested that language development by the age of one is often considered a "wellness" indicator of a young child's development progress. Learning to speak and use language throughout a child's growth is contingent upon a wide range of factors like listening, language development, social cues, comprehension, reasoning skills, attention, memory functions, word knowledge and proper grammar. All of those influence how well a child will be able to read or write.

And so we learn how to articulate through talking. We express our emotions through talking. We give expression to our thoughts through talking. We give our needs, wants, and desires a voice through talking.

Unfortunately, there isn't as much focus on listening. Yet, it is one of the most important skills you can have. How well you listen has a major impact on your job effectiveness, and on the quality of your relationships with others and ultimately God.

If you want to get through the rest of this year, I've got to tell you like God told me while standing on a cliff in Port Deposit, Maryland, "Stop talking so much." I love God because He can be whatever you need him to be. If you need a mother, He can be that. If you need a friend, He can be that too. God is a gentleman. He's not rude. If you're talking, He's going to let you talk. You can go on and on, but He won't interrupt you because He has spiritual manners.

The problem is you keep talking about your problems, and God wants to talk about your promises. You keep talking about your past, and God wants to talk about your future. You keep talking about your critics, and God wants to show you new friends. You keep talking about your weaknesses, and God wants to be your strength. You keep talking about your needs, and God wants to be your supply. You keep talking about your sickness, and God wants to talk about healing. You keep talking about your sin, and God wants to talk about his mercy. You keep talking about your boyfriend, and God wants to talk about your husband.

Remember, God gave us two ears and only one mouth for a reason ... to listen more and talk less. Listening is a prerequisite for learning. In other words, your next level tomorrow is contingent upon how well you listen today. God speaks to us through our minds and hearts, but sometimes we can't hear him because we are too distracted. So, we keep praying the same prayer when God has already answered it. You think He's ignoring you, but He's already answered you. You didn't hear him because you were still talking.

You don't have to wait until December 31st for the ball to drop. God is already doing a new thing. If you're always talking, you're going to miss his directives, goals, and objectives!

Your strategy, peace, strength, victory, deliverance, assurance, comfort, encouragement, and healing is waiting for you in a quiet place. Just like "hallelujah" and "thank you Jesus" are your weapons, so silence is your weapon. God is ready to talk, but He wants to know if you are ready to listen.

**Let us pray**.
*I recognize today, that you God, are worthy of all honor, praise and worship. I ask that you release the fullness of your Holy Spirit in my mind, body and soul. I ask, in the name of Jesus, that you forgive me of all my sins. I want to apologize today, for not being a better listener.*

*If I were honest, there have been times when I was talking while you were talking. There have been times when I slept while you were talking. There have been times when I turned away while you were talking. There have been times when I was planning while you were talking. There have been times when I rolled my eyes at you while you were talking.*

*God I am so sorry. Thank you for listening to me, even when I didn't listen to you! Thank you for not putting me in eternal time out. I come today craving your voice. I want you to know that I*

*live for your opinion. I want you to know that I can't make it with-*
*out your information, instruction, or revelation.*

*I ask, in the name of Jesus, that you show me how to quiet the*
*noises of my life. Unclog my ears. Allow me to hear you like never*
*before. Rebuke all infirmities, afflictions, inflammation, sickness*
*and disease in your people. I thank you for the power that you*
*gave me to decree and declare a thing. So, I decree and declare*
*that during the next 30 days I am going to see your miracles, signs,*
*and wonders. Amen.*

## My Challenge to You

It is my prayer today that God will arrest your tongue for the next seven days.  It is my prayer that you will seek and create ways to shut out and shut off all of the noises in your life, such as the cell phone, computer, radio, and television, for at least an hour a day.  Then sit in the presence of God.  Maybe start out by driving to work with your radio turned off.  Try getting up earlier for your own personal worship time, and have a journal handy so you don't miss what God is saying.  I know it's going to be uncomfortable at first because we are so attached to noise,  but those noises are distracting you from the voice of God. Shut them off.  Your victory depends on what you hear.

# Put Your Hands Up

"The fear of the Lord is the beginning of wisdom, and knowledge of the Holy One is understanding." Proverbs 9:10 NIV

In Little Rock, Arkansas, police received a call around 8:30 p.m. regarding a disturbance. Allegedly, two brothers got into an argument over money, and one brother got so angry that he went into the front yard and fired a gun into the air.

The police say the two brothers separated, but the one with the gun ran back into the house. Police then evacuated nearby homes and businesses as a safety precaution. They believed the man may have been under the influence of alcohol and narcotics. Officers' attempts to make contact were unsuccessful. After five grueling hours and three cans of tear gas, the standoff ended when the suspect came out of the house choking, tears streaming down his cheeks, and both hands lifted straight up in the air.

Everyone from the mountain to the sea recognizes the lifting up of both hands in the air as a sign of surrender. Webster's Dictionary defines surrender as "to yield, to give up possession of upon compulsion or demand; as to agree to forgo." Surrender is one of the greatest acts of courage you can make on your spiritual journey. True surrender brings you beyond the limitations of yourself to depending on a power much greater than you.  Surrender turns you upside down, holding your feet to the sky and your head to the earth.  Surrender teaches you to rest your mind in the cradle of God's arms while asking him for greater guidance and support in every area of your life.

Whether we admit it or accept it, we suffer with the desire to control, fix, and maintain the things concerning our lives.  However, surrendering to God means that we relinquish control of our lives, our time, our careers, our kids, our finances, and our bodies, anything we consider "ours."  We are simply caretakers.

I suggest to you that many of the tests and trials that you have endured thus far were not designed to destroy you, but they were designed to put you in a posture of surrender.  There are too many unemployed angels sitting around bored because you won't give up the things that have been assigned to them to handle. God cares about you and what you are going through, and He wants to carry your burdens.  God wants to carry your problems.  God wants to carry your heartbreak, disappointments, and fears. You keep walking around with the world on your shoulders, and your breakthrough is on the other side of surrender.  You want peace today?  You want your sleep back?  You want your smile back?  You want your joy back?  You want your fight back?  Put your hands up.

Give God total control of your life.  Not just one-third of it.  Not just half of it.  Not just your past but also your present.  Not just your body but also your mind.  Not just your kids but also your marriage.  Not just your singleness but also your dating. Not just your career but also your finances.  Not just your home but also your dreams.  Not just your family but also your friends.  Don't just stand there; put your hands up.  You can't, but God can.

**Let us pray.**

*I come today God saying: "All to Jesus, I surrender. All to you I freely give."*

*I don't want to carry these things anymore. The weight of what I have been facing is killing my hopes, my faith, and my peace. I am making a list today and checking it twice of everything I am giving to you.*

*I surrender all to Jesus. I surrender all of my heartache, grief, fears, and frustrations. I surrender my plans for yours. I surrender my will for your will. I surrender my ways for your ways. I surrender confusion for your peace. I surrender mourning for joy. I surrender my strategy for your voice. I surrender my ears for your direction. I surrender my eyes for your miracles. I surrender my heart for cleansing. My heart is filled with praise, and my hands are lifted in surrender because I know I can depend on you.*

*Thank you for being my God. Thank you for being reliable. Thank you for not turning your back on me. Thank you for loving me when I didn't love you. Thank you for not allowing the storms of life to kill me. I could be dead, sleeping in my grave, but you made the enemy behave. Thank you for keeping my mind and protecting me. Thank you for lifting up my head. Thank you for hearing and answering my prayers. You deserve my praise. I know that in you I live, breathe, move, and have my being.*

*I surrender my finances, household, mind, family, body, and heart. I come decreeing and declaring today that you're great, and nothing is impossible for you. I thank you for renewing my strength. I thank you for the faith to do the impossible. Thank you for giving me a million dollar idea. Thank you for the vision to see the invisible. It's in the undisputed, undefeated name of Jesus I do pray. Amen.*

# I Owe God This

After 12 long years, Keisha Cooper's day had finally come. As hundreds of people packed the Florence Civic Center in South Carolina, Shannon Cooper and the entire Cooper family sat in anticipation. They were overwhelmed with joy and gladness. As Keisha walked across the stage to accept her high school diploma from the Florence High School the family cheered and clapped for her.

What should have been the happiest day of their lives and what should have been a day filled with good times, good food, good fun, and good memories turned into one of their saddest days. Ten minutes after Keisha accepted her high school diploma, her mother Shannon was handcuffed, arrested and charged with disorderly conduct.

The South Carolina authorities maintained that Shannon's cheering was so loud it prohibited other parents from hearing their children's names. After being humiliated, processed, and released from the Florence County Detention Center, Shannon told a reporter as tears streamed down her face, "I'm sorry if I broke any rules, but you don't understand. I owe my daughter that praise. After all the odds she defied I owe her that praise. After all the tests she studied for I owe her that praise. After all the papers she wrote I owe her that praise." We're always talking about what God owes us, but have you ever calculated what you owe God?

After all the tests you've passed you owe God praise. After all the odds you've defied you owe God praise. After all the tears He's dried you owe God praise. After all the ways He's made, you owe God praise. After all the doors He's opened you owe God praise. After all the doors He's closed, you owe God praise. After all the mistakes you've made you owe God praise. It may not have been easy, but God still deserves praise.

You may have shed some tears, but God still deserves praise. Remember this: It's not what's in your hand that's a threat; it's what's in your mouth. The enemy knows it's time for you to see what you are declaring. Think of the weapons that were formed against you that did not prosper. You owe God praise. You aren't anybody in the Kingdom until what's coming out of your mouth makes the devil mad. Give God praise.

**Let us pray.**
*Most gracious and loving God, I thank you for this day. It's a day I've never seen before and will not see again. I know it isn't by my own might or strength that I am here today. I realize that I am living this moment totally because of you. I thank you for your grace and your mercy. I thank you that when the enemy came in like a flood, you lifted a standard (Isaiah 59:19). I thank you for your love, kindness, and power.*

*God, it is in you that I live, move, breathe, and have my being. God, before I ask you for anything today, I pause to thank you for everything. When I look back over my life I realize that I owe you praise. When I look back over the things that could have taken me out of here, I owe you praise. When I look back at how I could have lost my mind, God I owe you praise. When I look at the odds that were stacked against me, God I owe you praise.*

*Thank you for never leaving me. Thank you for being the best Daddy ever. Thank you for taking care of me. Thank you for not ignoring me. Thank you for pitying every groan and wiping every tear. God, I believe you're able, but touch my unbelief. Arrest panic attacks and depression. Comfort the broken hearted. Deliver the bound. Give strength to the weak and weary. Revive broken relationships. Issue an Amber Alert for lost peace and the loss of sleep.*

*Now unto you God, who is able to do immeasurably more than I could ask, think, dream, or even imagine according to your power that is working within me. To you be the glory and power, in the undisputed, undefeated name of Jesus I do pray. Amen!*

# The Art of War

"From the days of John the Baptist until now, the kingdom of heaven has been subjected to violence, and violent people have been raiding it." Matthew 11:12 NIV

My good girlfriend is dating a gentleman that was recently deployed to Iraq. One night during dinner she confided in me her concerns about the distance between them. She indicated that they barely talk. When he is going to sleep she is getting up, and when she is going to bed he's getting up. When she writes him he writes back, but his letters are very short and concise. When she writes him she sends a card. The quality of their dialogue is at a minimum.

The Holy Spirit had me share with her: there is a mind set when you're at peace and one when you're at war. Peace is when there's harmony, serenity and tranquility. I reminded her that he is in a battle. He can't have the same disposition during a war that he had during the time of peace. When you're in war you're fighting for your life. You're fighting for your sanity. You don't have time to reply back to every email, return every call, or make every party.

The Art of War, attributed to the high-ranking Chinese military general, Sun Tzu, is one of the oldest and most successful and influential books on military strategy in the world. Likewise, if you want to win for the rest of this year you have to have a strategy for your victory.

You might have to get up a little earlier for morning devotions. You might have to pray a little harder, or skip a few meals. Wartime requires different sleeping, different eating, different praying, and different friends. Whether you know it or not, when you make up your mind to totally surrender your life to God a real demon – not the ghosts and goblins of Halloween – is assigned to take you out of here.

You need to have some tactics to keep your joy, a strategy to keep your peace, and positioning to keep your fight. This fight can't be won with tears, complaints, mace or a pocket knife. You need the Word of God. Paul said it this way, "For the weapons of our warfare are not carnal, but mighty through God to the pulling down of strongholds" (I Corinthians 10:4).

The enemy knows that when you pray and praise that you are getting the attention of God. Prayer and praise will change your condition. Prayer and praise will change your position. God will show up on your behalf.

Don't just stand there. Pull out your weapon. You've followed rules and procedures long enough. You've been a lady long enough. You've been politically-correct long enough. It's time to roll up your sleeves, and lay on your face in prayer. You may be broke, broken, depressed, sick, struggling or weak, but if you never declare war, you will never be able to declare victory.

**Let us pray.**

*Dear God: You knew about this battle before I was born. I refuse to be consumed with worry and fear because I trust you. Thank you for being a present help in my time of trouble. Do it God. In the name of Jesus I pray. Amen.*

# I Am Getting Through the Rest of This Year!

"As he went along, he saw a man blind from birth. His disciples asked him, Rabbi, who sinned, this man or his parents, that he was born blind?  Neither this man nor his parents sinned, said Jesus, but this happened so that the works of God might be displayed in him.  As long as it is day, we must do the works of him who sent me. Night is coming, when no one can work.  While I am in the world, I am the light of the world.  After saying this, he spit on the ground, made some mud with the saliva, and put it on the man's eyes.  Go, he told him, wash in the Pool of Siloam (this word means "Sent"). So the man went and washed, and came home seeing.  His neighbors and those who had formerly seen him begging asked, Isn't this the same man who used to sit and beg?  Some claimed that he was. Others said, No, he only looks like him.  But he himself insisted, I am the man.  How then were your eyes opened? they asked.  He replied, The man they call Jesus made some mud and put it on my eyes. He told me to go to Siloam and wash. So I went and washed, and then I could see."  John 9:1-11 NIV

Crawling or walking, smiling or crying, with or without you, I am getting through this.  No matter what year it is, I still believe that January 1st marks a new beginning. It's a fresh start, a new chapter, or a clean slate.  People from all walks of life are excited and pumped up to embrace the next 364 days with a renewed resolution, purpose and passion.

- Passion to lose those unwanted pounds
- Passion to turn off the TV and get in the gym
- Passion to get back into school
- Passion to start a new career
- Passion to study a little harder
- Passion to read the Bible more
- Passion to finally get it all together

We dust off the tennis shoes.  Buy a treadmill, and come up with a plan.  If you're like me, there's that time between your plans and your intentions when the snow starts melting; the birds start chirping; and the flowers start blooming. The treadmill becomes a clothesline, and the realities of life just happen.   It's not the devil. It's not me. It's just life. Things break.  Systems fail.  Tires go flat.  People change.  Storms come.  Bodies get sick.  It's just life.  It's what happens when you take 10 steps forward only to get knocked back 11.

I know I am among the Bible toters and scripture quoters, but I have had seasons when all I could say was "Lawd, really?!"  Who starts off the year believing they will lose their job?  Who starts off the year believing this will be the year for sickness?  What married couple starts off the year believing the marriage will end in divorce?  What homeowner starts off the year believing it will be the year for foreclosure?  What family starts off the year thinking this will be the year to pick out a casket?

I know what it's like to start off January with good intentions, a strategic plan, goals, and objectives. I also know what it's like to see them fizzle out over time.

It's easy to get caught up on a timeline and what hasn't happened yet. In between planning for the holidays and rooting for our favorite sports team, we start giving God the silent treatment. You don't have to write off the rest of the year because of your disappointments and frustrations. God isn't finished with you. Just because He's not talking doesn't mean He's not working.

This brings us to the text. It's a familiar story that can offer fresh insight on how to end the year. After almost being stoned to death, Jesus leaves the temple area. As Jesus is walking down the street, He sees this blind man. We don't know anything about the man except his condition. Though he could not see Jesus, Jesus could see him. To end the year strong, remember you have not been forgotten. You may not be able to see the Lord, but He sees you. He sees you and your condition.

To end the year strong, you also need to be in position. Be where you're supposed to be. If you're supposed to be at church, then be at church. If you're supposed to be at work at 7 a.m., then stop easing in at 7:15 a.m. If you're supposed to be at PTA, then be there. If you're supposed to be at the doctor's, then be there. If you're supposed to be home, then be there.

The text immediately presents a dilemma because the writer wants the reader to know this man's condition was from birth. The text mentions nothing about his name, age, or background. All we know is his condition was hopeless. It's one thing to go blind; it's another thing to be born blind. It's one thing to be depressed right now; it's another thing to have depression.

Can you imagine starting off the year naming it and claiming it, and ending the year in the same condition? Can you imagine declaring and decreeing but still not receiving?  The blind man was sitting at the intersection of another year still blind.  What about you?  Is this another year still single?  Another year still depressed?  Another year still sick?  Another year still broken.  Another year still hurt?

When an unprovoked Jesus shows up on the scene, He sees the man.  Nothing about the text says he asked for it.  Nothing about the text shows he prayed for it.  Nothing about the text shows he fasted for it.  God knows what you need, and He cares about what is disabling you.

I wondered about the blind man.  How do you desire something that you've never seen?  How do you see it before you see it?  How do you strive for great when everybody else seems to be settling for good?  How do you keep a smile when you feel like crying? How do you believe when everybody is laughing at your dreams?  How do you keep moving when you feel like you're stuck?  How do you pick up your head when it's been down so long?

The man spoke from the text: "You've got to have faith that the street you are on is not your last stop, and you got to have the strength to wash the mud off your eyes. God saw me."

In the beginning of the passage the man was blind. By the end of the passage he had sight.  God sees what's disabling you. Wash off the mud of your past, the mud of your disappointments, and the mud of your frustration. Get moving. Get back in the game.  Your destiny depends on it.  You may have to cry, but make a declaration.  You may have to crawl, but make a declaration.  The year is not over. The street you are on is not your last stop.

# I Will Recover from This

"David inquired of the Lord, saying, Shall I pursue this band? Shall I overtake them? And He said to him, Pursue, for you will surely overtake them, and you will surely rescue all." I Samuel 30:8 NIV

Shortly after he took the oath of office, the world stopped as President Barack Obama gave his first official State of the Union Address before the United States Congress and the anxious American public. Millions of people watched as the President made his 12-letter, five-syllable, three-word declaration: "**I will recover**." For the rest of this year, stop letting people read the last rites over your future. Declare, "I will recover. Standing or crawling, I will recover." I don't know what you've lost. I don't know how long it's been gone. All I know is it's time to start declaring your recovery.

REGAIN, RETRIEVE, RECLAIM, AND REPOSSESS!!!

You may not know how or when. It may not look like it or feel like it now, but the President made an outward declaration over the nation. We will recover. If you've never lost anything, then this recovery may mean absolutely nothing to you. However, there is a remnant of people in this country – and even reading this book – that can testify what it means to experience great loss. Some have lost sleep. Some have lost joy. Some have lost dreams. Some have lost strength. Some have lost incomes. Some have lost loved ones.

If you are a part of the remnant, then I have a State of Union Address for you. Just like the recovery that takes place after a natural disaster, it's time for you to recover. After the earth stops shaking, winds stop blowing, rains stop falling, and trees stopped breaking, you've got to get up, brush off your shoulders, and hold a press conference in your bedroom. Make the announcement to all the powers here, in heaven and in hell that you will recover.

Not some of, not a little bit, not most of it, but absolutely all of it! If you have to recover alone you will recover. If you've got to change your number you will recover. If you've got to get counseling you will recover. If you've got to give some relationships a two-week notice, you will recover. If you've got to eat lunch alone you will recover.

For the rest of this year, stop allowing people to eulogize your destiny, and start declaring and decreeing, "**I will recover**." Tweet it. Text it. Email it. Hum it. Sing it. "**I will recover**."

# I Know Who Did It

"He replied, Whether he is a sinner or not, I don't know. One thing I do know. I was blind but now I see!" John 9:25 NIV

I love A&E's The First 48. It is an action packed series that takes viewers behind the scenes of real-life investigations as homicide detectives try to solve murder cases in the critical first 48 hours. The series follows the nation's top police departments and homicide detectives in Charlotte, Miami, Louisville, Alabama, and Texas. As the investigation unfolds, viewers have unprecedented access to crime scenes, interrogations, and forensic processing.

"For homicide detectives, the clock starts ticking the moment they are called to the crime scene, because their chance of solving the case is cut in half if they don't get a lead in the first 48 hours."

Each passing hour gives the suspect more time to flee, witnesses more time to forget what they saw, and crucial evidence more time to become lost or compromised.

Sometimes all the detectives have is the body, and sometimes all they have is the weapon. They may not have a clue about the perpetrator. Then all of a sudden the phone rings, and the caller says, "I know who did it. I saw the whole thing." If you've ever watched the show, you know they never show the eyewitnesses' faces for their own safety. The testimony of a witness is valuable and often the key information that convicts the criminal. Repeating what you've heard is called hearsay, but seeing with your own eyes is called witnessing.

In other words, it's one thing to hear that God is a keeper. It's another thing to actually be kept by God. It's one thing to hear that God is a healer. It's another thing to actually be healed by God. That's why the enemy is so mad with some of you this year. You have survived, and he knows that you're going to tell your story. He knows that he is defeated in two ways: by the blood of the Lamb and by the word of your testimony. This brings us to the heart of our conversation.

Within the first 48 hours of receiving his miracle, the man was called in and interrogated. You would have thought people would have been happy for him, but they weren't. They called him downtown for questioning. They asked him about his miraculous healing. They questioned him about Jesus. "Was He a sinner or not?" "Where did He go?" The blind man said, "I really don't know. One thing is for certain. I was blind, but now I see."

If you really want to get through the rest of this year, Thanksgiving can't be just another day off for you. It's got to be an attitude and a lifestyle because you are evidence of God's handiwork. You are the evidence that God is who He says He is. You are the evidence that God's still able to do what He says He can do. You are the evidence that God's still writing the pages of the New Testament. How dare you sit on what you saw. You can't sit on what God has done for you. You can't sit on the doors that God has opened for you.

What have you witnessed? What's your testimony? Did God dry your tears? Did He keep your mind? Did God restore your praise? Did God restore your motivation? Did He restrain your tongue?

Did He turn your mourning into joy? Did God pull you back from a breakdown? Did He save you from destruction?

Thanksgiving is also a time to celebrate survival. It has nothing do with the turkey or sweet potato pie. Through many dangers, toils, and snares you made it, and God did it. Pat yourself on the back, and give yourself a high five. Send yourself some flowers. This is a time for you to look in the rearview mirror of your life, and give God a "flashback" praise.

Do you know who did it for you? Do you know who saved you? Do you know who has kept you? Do you know who lifted up your head and dried your tears? It was God! Sing it on the metro train or in the line at the store. It was God! It was God! You are not that strong or that wise. It was God. He did it. That's why you have to have an attitude of gratitude because it was God in spite of you. It was God. I know who did it.

**Let us pray.**
*Gracious and merciful God, I come to you on a day that I have never seen before and will never see again. I come into your presence with a mouth full of praise and a heart full of thanksgiving. I come declaring "I will bless thee oh Lord." I come declaring and decreeing that you are my source and supply. It is in you God that I live, move, breathe, and have my being.*

*I thank you for making a way out of no way. I thank you for blessing me, even when I didn't understand the mud and the spit. I thank you for telling me yes, and I also thank you for telling me no. I recognize and realize that you are God and God alone. I ask that you will release the fullness of your Holy Spirit in my mind, body and soul. I come recognizing that you have been a shelter for me all year long. Though seasons change your love and power remain constant. For that God I am grateful.*

I ask, in the name of Jesus, that you forgive me of all of my sins. I ask, in the name of Jesus, that you rebuke all infirmities, afflictions, sickness, and disease in your people. God this is a tough time for many people. I know you to be a God of comfort. I ask right now, in the name of Jesus, that you overwhelm their hearts, minds and souls with your compassion, gentleness and comfort. You promised to heal broken hearts.

You promised to give us beauty for ashes. You promised to give us the oil of joy for our mourning. You promised to give us the garment of praise for the spirit of heaviness. You promised if we sowed in tears we would reap in joy. Give us a super dose of your hope and strength in the midst of it all. Give us power in the middle of the pain. Give us a peace that surpasses all human understanding. Give us a glimpse of your table.

For those with loved ones in prison, God be with them and their families. You have given me keys to the Kingdom of Heaven, and whatever I bind and loose on earth shall be bound and loosed in heaven. I ask you to loose your angels in great abundance into the prisons and into the cells. Give their families a blessed assurance that you're a starter and finisher. Even prison cells can't keep out your love, mercy, and grace.

God help me to figure out how to be thankful when I have lost so much this year. Speak to my heart today. Speak directly to my disappointment and frustration with you. Renew my strength. Renew my power to believe again. Renew my power to dream again. Renew my power to love again. In Jesus' name. Amen.

# Greatness Attracts Trouble

"For if the readiness is present, it is acceptable according to what a person has, not according to what he does not have." II Corinthians 8:12

After two years of being off of the center court, Serena Williams made her return at Wimbledon in a match against Aggie Radwanska. Though a few years younger than Serena, Aggie gave the tennis veteran a run for her money. The match went into three sets. By the middle of the second set, the commentators had almost written off Serena. But, she navigated the third set with power, precision, and passion, securing her fifth Wimbledon title and joining the ranks of her sister Venus Williams, who also holds five Wimbledon titles.

I know that's what you expect from the Compton born and bred tennis pro. That's what I expect too, but when Serena accepted her title she said something that stopped me in my tracks. She said, "I am amazed to be here today because just two years ago I was lying on my couch depressed, and I thought I would never play tennis again." She went on to say, "I was recovering from two different surgeries and developed blood clots in both of my lungs. I was in so much pain that it hurt to walk. I wasn't thinking about tennis; all I wanted to do was live."

Life is full of ups and downs.  Serena's "downs" may not be yours, but we all have them. Greatness doesn't exempt you from trouble; it attracts it.  If your destiny is great, your trouble will be great. I get sick of people who think they're going to float through life without troubles. If that were true, Jesus wouldn't have told us "in this life you will have trouble." I like to talk to people who are fighting a good fight of faith in the midst of it all. I like to talk to people who have learned to take a licking and keep on ticking. I wanted to talk to an expert on the subject, so I consulted the Apostle Paul. I asked him, "What do you do when the storms of life are raging fiercely against you? What do you do when your heart is torn with pain?"  Paul said, "We are hard pressed on every side, but not crushed; perplexed but not in despair, persecuted, but not abandoned, struck down, but not destroyed" (2 Corinthians 4:8).

I know this season has been tough,  but you're still here.  The fact that you're still here means it's not over.  There's still a champion in you.  I don't care what storms are raging; no storm can last forever.  Your problems can't cancel God's promises.  Your best stories won't come from your successes but from your struggles. And the seeds from your success will come from your failures. Your praise will be birthed from your pain.  Hold on.  Hold out. You've come too far to give up.  These setbacks are only setups for your comeback.

**Let us pray.**
*All wise and loving God, I come today with my hands lifted up and my mouth filled with praise because you've been that good.  God before I ask you for anything, I must stop and thank you for everything.  Thanks for keeping me, protecting me, making ways for me, opening doors for me, and keeping my mind.  Thank you for the birds and the bees.  Thank you for the sun and the moon.  Thank you for the mountains and the oceans.  Thank you for keeping me. Thank you for protecting my family.  Thank you for not allowing me to lose my mind.*

*God, I am calling on you with all types of situations, diagnoses, and circumstances. I come declaring and decreeing, that trials have come on every hand, yet I still feel like going on.*

*I don't have all of the answers, but I still feel like going on. I don't know when it's going to happen, but I still feel like going on. Even though my options are few, I still feel like going on. Sometimes, it seems like the odds are against me, but I still feel like going on. Thank you for being everything to me. Thank you for reminding me today that you see me and what I am going through. Thank you today for being the source of my strength and the strength of my life. Thank you for reminding me today that nothing is impossible for you.*

*Thank you today for canceling the plot that the enemy had for me. Thank you today for destroying every yolk and stronghold. Thank you for canceling generational curses. Thank you today for giving me power to tread on the enemy. Thank you for giving me vision to see the invisible and see the impossible. Thank you for keeping me when trouble comes my way.*

*Give me the serenity to accept the things, people, and circumstances that I cannot change. Give me the courage to change the things that I can, and give me the priceless wisdom to know the difference. In Jesus' name I pray. Amen.*

# You Won't Break

"He gives strength to the weary and increases the power of the weak." Isaiah 40:29 NIV

Her mother said from the time she first opened her mouth, it was obvious she was bound for greatness. Singing in her church choir Sunday after Sunday, she had aspirations of being a back up singer just like her mother. By her teens she was already singing background for Chaka Khan and Lou Rawls. After spending a few years developing her abilities and making industry contacts, she was finally ready for the big time. By her 18th birthday she had already signed a management contract.

In 1985, Whitney Houston signed with Arista Records. Her self-titled debut album spun off three number one singles: "Saving All My Love for You," "How Will I Know," and "The Greatest Love of All." She graced the covers of Seventeen and Glamour magazines, but she didn't know her own strength. She toured the world, drove the best cars, and ate at the best restaurants, but she didn't know her own strength. Her godmother was Aretha Franklin, but she still didn't know her own strength.

We've got more education than our ancestors, but do we know our own strength? We've got more technology than any other generation, but do we know our strength? We've got bigger churches with more seats, but do we know our own strength? We have leather seats and navigation systems in our cars, but do we know our own strength? We've got more pairs of shoes than feet to wear them, but do we know our own strength? We've got access to so much more, but do we know our own strength?

Let me remind you:

- Your strength is not in your possessions.
- Your strength is not in your position.
- Your strength is not in your looks.
- Your strength is not in your degrees.
- Your strength is not in your bank account.
- Your strength is not in your affiliations.
- Your strength is not in your significant other.
- Your strength is in God.

The reason it's been so hard this year is God has been whipping you into shape. I know you thought the pressure and weight were going to kill you, but you are being toned. You are being stretched. You are building muscle. "These present sufferings cannot be compared to the glory that shall be revealed" (Romans 8:18). In other words, your suffering qualifies you for an upgrade. Jeremiah says it this way, "If you have raced with men on foot and they have worn you out, how can you compete with horses?

If you stumble in safe country, how will you manage in the forest?" (Jeremiah 12:5). In other words, if you can't get a prayer through on a good day, you won't be able to get one through on a rough one. If you can't be a good steward in an apartment, you will never be able to be a good steward in a house. If you're not an honest employee, you won't be an honest employer.

I know there were times this year that you thought it would be the end of you. I know you felt like giving up. I know you felt like God was punishing you. I know you thought you wouldn't make it. I am here to tell you God wants you to tap into your strength. You don't know your own strength. You're stronger than you know. You can't crash; you can't tumble. God won't let you crumble. You have survived your darkest hour. Your faith kept you alive. Hold your head up high. The devil can huff and puff, but you won't break.

**Let us pray.**
*Awesome and amazing God, I come to you today because no other help I know. If you turn your face from me, Lord where will I go? Great is your mercy, your loving kindness, and your tender mercies. You are forever faithful toward me. Great is your grace. Lord I come today, just giving you back your word.*

*Your Word declares that I can, "Ask and it will be given, seek and you fill find, knock and the door will be opened" (Matthew 7:7). God I am coming to you asking, seeking, and knocking. I am petitioning you God like never before because my very existence depends on you. I need you Jesus! I am desperate for fresh manna. I need my worry to collide with your Word. I need my problems to collide with your promises. I need my weakness to collide with your strength. I need my storms to collide with your peace. I need my lack to collide with your overflow. I need my sickness to collide with your healing. I need my disappointment to collide with my destiny. I need my sins to collide with your mercy. I need my feet to collide with your direction. I need my tongue to collide with your heart. I need my mind to collide with your comfort. I need my heartache to collide with your comfort. I need my pain to collide with your power. I need my family to collide with your protection.*

*God you are the source of my strength. You are the strength of my life. In Jesus' name I pray. Amen.*

# That's All I Needed to Know

"Opening his mouth, Peter said: I most certainly under-stand now that God is not one to show partiality." Acts 10:34 NIV

We all read the story. We all saw it on the news, but I had to find out about the man for myself. From the onset, one would have thought his father was a banker from Wall Street and his mother was a "Real Housewife of Beverly Hills." In reality, David Ruben-stein grew up in the Park Heights section of West Baltimore City. His father was a retired postal worker and his mother a home-maker. Rubenstein lived an insulated life. He attended Baltimore public schools, and was accepted into Duke University. He relied on scholarships to fund his education.

Graduating at the top of his class, he went on to the University of Chicago's Law School. His resume is impressive, and his col-leagues say he is a workaholic who rarely sleeps and hasn't missed a day of work since 1973. Rubenstein said he reads eight books a month and five newspapers a day.

In addition to being the CEO of one of the country's most success-ful businesses, he is a husband and a father. Thirty years ago he didn't have money for his college tuition, but today he can afford to give a $7.5 million gift to the National Park Service to repair the National Monument.

Thirty years ago, he was just a number. Today he is number 139 on Forbes list of 400 richest Americans. I don't know about you, but that's all I need to know. I thank God that His power is not exclusive. Sometimes I need a reminder that God still has the power to make ordinary people extraordinary. Sometimes I need a reminder that God still has the power to take our good and make it great. This scripture is tailored to teach and remind us that God doesn't play favorites.

I don't know what your specific needs are, but the Lord is the owner of it all. He specializes in transforming the ordinary into extraordinary. He can change people, situations, issues, conditions and circumstances. There is nothing He can't do. If He can take a man from the financial aid line to the major donors' line, He can do it for you.

You've got to see it before you see it. See yourself whole. See yourself debt free. See your relationship restored. See yourself happy. See yourself as the head and not the tail. See yourself as the lender and not the borrower. God needs your participation. Don't just stand there. It's too early in the game to be defeated. Tie up your shoestrings. There is more to you than what meets the eye. I don't care where you started off. God has invested greatness into you, and He expects a return on his investment. You can't die. You can't quit. You've got to get your head back in the game. Believe that greatness, great things, and great blessings are not for an exclusive group of people. Tell yourself it's on.

**Let us pray.**
*God it's me again. It's in you that I live, move, breathe and have my being. God, I come today because I know that nothing moves you faster than your Word and my faith. I come today completely*

*desperate for you because I recognize that I am nothing without you. I can't do anything without you.*

*Your Word declares that "If my people who are called by my name, humble themselves and pray, and seek my face and turn from their wicked ways, then will I hear from heaven, forgive their sin and heal their land" (2 Chronicles 7:14).*

*God, I am calling, praying, seeking, and repenting. I need you to heal my land. I need you to heal my heart. I need you to heal my body. I need you to heal my mind. I need you to heal my family. I need you to heal my church. I need you to heal my community. I need you to heal this nation.*

*I thank you for how you've brought me through and for what you are bringing me to. I thank you for revelation, confirmation, and affirmation. Thank you for meeting me in prayer day after day, week after week, month after month.*

*In you there is nothing broken and nothing missing. Please restore my missing peace, joy, strength, will, determination, dreams, sleep, money, self-esteem, self-worth, resilience, perseverance, hope and faith.*

*I come in expectation that this is going to be the year of "show and tell." I will be a bold witness of your mighty acts. Thank you for giving me the strength, power and wisdom to take life one day at a time. You are truly the best thing that ever happened to me. Please don't stop until you finish the work that you started in me. In the name of Jesus. Amen.*

# Stop Going Out of the House Half Dressed

"Finally, be strong in the Lord and in his mighty power. Put on the full armor of God, so that you can take your stand against the devil's schemes. For our struggle is not against flesh and blood, but against the rulers, against the authorities, against the powers of this dark world and against the spiritual forces of evil in the heavenly realms." Ephesians 6:10-17 NIV

Studies show that Americans are working more. And even when we are not at work, we spend countless hours still thinking about work. If you add the commute time to the equation, we may spend more time going to work, being at work, or coming home from work than we do anything else. For at least five days out of seven, we go to a place where we are paid to perform some task. We then take our wages and pay rent, buy groceries, put gas in the car, and meet our other financial responsibilities.

Unsurprisingly, the workplace is a major source of stress for many. It has become so painful; it's almost like going to the dentist's office. The instant you pull up, your heart starts racing, your palms start sweating, and you go numb because you don't want to feel the hurt and pain. Before we even get to work we have to go through the morning routine. That may mean getting kids ready for school, grabbing breakfast, and navigating rush hour traffic whether in a car or on public transportation. Once at work, we must endure the fear of furloughs and downsizing, and the pressure of meeting unrealistic deadlines in a hostile environment. Then there are all the isms: racism, classism, sexism, etc.

Your assignment for the next few weeks is to encourage yourself slam in the middle of your workplace. Reconsider what you do, how you do it, and why you do it.

First, stress can kill you. You've got to make up in your mind that your job will not be a major source of stress. Just like people take cigarette breaks, take intentional prayer breaks. Go for walks on nice days. Steal away, and spend your lunch with God. Add some type of exercise to your daily routine either before, during or after the work day. It's a good stress buster. If you think your stress requires the help of a trained professional, check with your employer about assistance. Every workplace should have some sort of Employee Assistance Program (EAP).

Secondly, you've got to stop going to work half dressed. You've got on a St. John suit, but you're naked. You've got on red bottom pumps, but you're naked. You've got your makeup bag, but your Bible is at home. You're naked. Your hair is done, nails are done, but you have no Word in your heart. You're naked.

This scripture is tailored to teach us what we should have on before we leave the house. The belt of truth is when you know and apply God's Word. The breastplate of righteousness is the integrity and truth in your personal life. Somebody has to operate in truth in your office; let it be you.

The gospel of peace is carrying the good news in your heart. Find a scripture and make it yours, so when things get crazy you can stay relaxed.

The shield of faith is your confidence in the Lord and His Word. No matter what it looks like your confidence is in the Lord.

The helmet of salvation is the certainty of your victory. It's your assurance that if God be for you, who can be against you.

The sword of the Spirit is the Word of God. You will go back home for your cell phone. Having your Bible and other inspirational books is just as vital.

Prayer is not mentioned as a part of the armor, but we need to acknowledge its power in our lives. Don't leave home without.

## Put Things in Perspective

You are not there because of your resume. You are not there because of your networking. You are not there to organize the potlucks and baby showers. You are not there for the health insurance.

Can you keep a secret? You are an undercover agent. God has you there for a reason. You are on an assignment to advance Jesus. You're on assignment, so your coworkers don't bust hell wide open. Just like you have a job, the enemy has a job. Stop getting so blown away when he shows his face in your workplace. It is your job to change the atmosphere. It's your job to let your light shine. It's your job to love the hell out of people.

In Christendom, we get it confused because we think only the people in the pulpit are required to do full-time ministry. That's not true. Whether you negotiate contracts, write tickets, answer phones, fix hair, or scrub toilets, you are in full-time ministry. We have different titles, different tasks, different work locations, but we all work for the same CEO. Our boss is God and our assignment is the Kingdom. You are literally the hands and feet of God.

So, remember:

- The enemy doesn't want your promotion he wants your life.
- The enemy doesn't want your office he wants your joy.
- The enemy doesn't want your pension he wants your promise.

You can forget your lunch. You can forget your cell phone. You can forget to spray on perfume in the morning. But, you can't go to work half dressed. Stop playing with the enemy; he's trying to wipe you out. He knows he can't get you in the club, so he's waiting for you on your job.

You've got to put on the full armor of God. Without it you're a sitting duck. Pick up your head. Dust off your shoulders. You're going from good to great this year and that includes in the workplace.

**Let us pray.**
*God it's me again. God it is in you that I live, move, breathe, and have my being. God, I come today because what I need exceeds my capacity. I come today completely desperate for you. I recognize that I am nothing without you. I realize that I can do nothing without you.* •

*Your Word declares, that "If my people who are called by name, humble, themselves and pray and seek my face and turn from their wicked ways, then will I hear from heaven, forgive their sin, and heal their land" (2 Chronicles 7:14). God, I am calling, praying, seeking, and repenting. I need you to heal my land. Heal this land. Heal hearts. Heal bodies. Heal minds. Heal families. Heal churches. Heal communities. Heal this nation.*

*Renew our strength. Thank you for how you brought me through. Thank you for revelation. Thank you for confirmation. Thank you for affirmation. Thank you for meeting me in the workplace day after day, week after week, month after month. Thank you for giving me the strength, power, and wisdom to take one day at a time.  You are truly the best thing that ever happened to me. Please don't stop until you finish the work that you started in me. In Jesus' name. Amen.*

## It's Crunch Time

"We are afflicted in every way, but not crushed; perplexed, but not despairing; persecuted, but not forsaken; struck down, but not destroyed" II Corinthians 4:8-9 NIV

Usher is not the only one making confessions; I have a confession too. My confession is: I am not much of a sports enthusiast. However, every now and then something about football captures my complete and undivided attention ... mainly halftime. I enjoy the festivities. I enjoy watching the radical fans. I enjoy the performances. I enjoy the commentators.

The thing that I love the most during halftime is when the reporters give the fans an all-access-pass into the locker room. As the coach huddles with the players off the field for a few moments, the players also have time to regroup, refocus and renew their commitment to winning the game.

Today I come as your Holy Ghost cheerleader. This devotion serves as our huddle. You may have entered this huddle unemployed, underemployed, or bruised. You may be frustrated, tired, overwhelmed, or fed up. I am here to remind you that no matter where you are on the field of life, how you play in the red zone will determine how your year will end.

102

It's crunch time.  Renew your will to win.  The clock is ticking.  The heavens are cheering, and  God still reigns with all dominion and power.  Pick up your head.  Brush off your shoulders.  Tie up your cleats.  Dry your eyes.  The game is not over.  Pray like God is listening.  Run like God is blocking.  Smile like God is making a way.  Sleep like God is working it out.

Don't give up.  Don't give in.  Don't throw in the towel.  Get off that bench.  Shoot for the hoop.  Run for the goal.  I don't care how many fouls you have had.  I don't care about who or what is blocking you.  I don't care about what the score looks like.  You can make it.  You're more than a conqueror.  God didn't bring you this far to leave you.

# Laughing at My Pain

"Blessed are you who hunger now, for you shall be satisfied. Blessed are you who weep now, for you shall laugh."
Luke 6:21 NIV

Some time ago, I went to see comedian Kevin Hart's movie, Laugh at my Pain. Cussing aside, I give the movie four and a half stars. For one hour and twenty minutes, funnyman Hart headlines his own comedy tour from the amazing Nokia Theatre in Los Angeles, California. After seeing the movie I had a better understanding of why this movie is so popular. Hart's gut wrenching humor left me totally amazed and wanting more. During his routine no topic was off limits. He talked about his childhood, his feisty mother, his drug addicted father, his children, and his messy divorce. Chronicling his humble and painful beginnings, the comedian gives the viewer an intimate front row seat into the cabinet of his soul and shares how he's learned to laugh at his pain.

We walked to the car still laughing and trying to mimic a few of the comedian's lines. As the laughter turned to silence and we headed home, my thoughts drifted to a conversation with my grandmother, Chick Brown. She told me: "Baby, sometimes you've got to laugh to keep from crying."

I really hadn't lived enough life to ask her how you can laugh at what makes you cry. How do you laugh when you're hurting? How do you laugh when you're struggling? How do you laugh when you feel like giving up?

Then all of a sudden, the Holy Spirit jumped into my conversation and said, "In all of your getting Akisha Sharon Greene, I need you to get there are 42 references to laughter in the Bible." The Bible teaches there are times to weep and times to laugh. Abraham laughed. Sarah laughed. And, God laughed. Yes, the creator of all things, laughed. If you go through the Bible, then you will see that He never laughed just to laugh. He laughed at the enemy. He laughed at the plan of the enemy. He laughed at the enemy's tactics and schemes. And, God laughed at the enemy's minions and attacks.

There is a lesson there. If you want to get through the rest of this year, start laughing at the devil's schemes and tricks. Let your outward laugh be confirmation of an inward peace. Let it be a declaration of your inward confidence. Your outward laugh tells the devil he's defeated. Your outward laugh says the blood of Jesus still works. Your outward laugh says the Lord is mighty in battle. Your outward laugh says you shall not want because the Lord is your shepherd.

The more hell you experience the louder your laugh should be. The more pain you feel the louder your laugh should be. Learn how to laugh when nobody is telling a joke. Learn how to laugh while tears are streaming down your face. Blessed are you who weep now, for you shall have the last laugh.

**Let us pray.**
*Great is your mercy toward me. Your loving kindness toward me. Your tender mercies toward me. Day after day. Great is your grace.*

*Oh God, my God, all to thee I owe. I thank you God that before my feet even hit the floor this morning, you had already made a direct deposit into my life's account with everything I need. I thank you that your Word declares that your mercies are new every morning. I thank you for not giving me stale grace or stale mercy. God, I may not be able to depend on anything or anyone else, but I can always count on, lean on and depend on you.*

*God, I ask you today to finish what you started. Bless me indeed. Don't allow me to finish praying feeling the same way that I started. Heal where there is sickness. Deliver where there is bondage. Give hope to the hopeless. Give joy to the joyless. Give strength to the weary. Give comfort to the grieving. Make bitter people better. Thank you for the power to laugh again. Thank you for the power to live again. Thank you for the power to love again. I love you Jesus! Amen.*

# Who Told You That?

"But from the fruit of the tree which is in the middle of the garden, God has said, You shall not eat from it or touch it, or you will die. The serpent said to the woman, You surely will not die! For God knows that in the day you eat from it your eyes will be opened, and you will be like God, knowing good and evil. When the woman saw that the tree was good for food, and that it was a delight to the eyes, and that the tree was desirable to make one wise, she took from its fruit and ate; and she gave also to her husband with her, and he ate. Then the eyes of both of them were opened, and they knew that they were naked; and they sewed fig leaves together and made themselves loin coverings. They heard the sound of the Lord God walking in the garden in the cool of the day, and the man and his wife hid themselves from the presence of the Lord God among the trees of the garden. Then the Lord God called to the man, and said to him, Where are you? He said, I heard the sound of You in the garden, and I was afraid because I was naked; so I hid myself. And He said, Who told you that you were naked? Have you eaten from the tree of which I commanded you not to eat?" Genesis 3:3-11 NIV

With the evolution of cable and high definition TV, the Internet, cell phones, digital music, chat rooms, and social media, we are right in the middle of the information age. Information is facts, intelligence, knowledge, notices, news, reports, or data provided about something or someone.

That's how our military family was able to capture Osama Bin Laden in May 2011 because our President received intelligence on his location. In this day and time, you have to know that the right information can get you to the right place at the right time. The wrong information will cause you to get lost.

That's also how the President was able to make a decision from Washington, DC, about a situation in Kabul, Afghanistan. He was presented with data that had already been inspected, transmitted, collected, and processed by a military information specialist.

If you want to get through the rest of this year, you better start acting like an information specialist. After all you've experienced, you should have some data on God. After all of the tears you've cried, you should have some knowledge of God. After all you've seen you should have some intelligence on God. After all of the bills He's paid, and all of the ways He's made, you should have collected and processed some information on God. With all of that data, knowledge, and intelligence, you've got to watch out for the snakes that are telling you that you're naked. You've got to watch out for the snakes that are telling you to quit or give up.

A snake is any person, any thought, any information, any report, or any data that is contrary to the Word and promises of God. If you want to get through the rest of this year then you have got to stop listening to snakes.

Remember what God has already done. Remember what God has already promised. You've seen God's healing, experienced his provision, and witnessed his deliverance. You have the data, the facts, knowledge and intelligence. If He's moved in the past, He will move in the present. Don't let snakes trick you into doubting or questioning the promises and plan of God. Always check the source.

- Who told you that you would always be broke?
- Who told you that you would always be single?
- Who told you that you would always struggle?
- Who told you that you would always be unemployed?
- Who told you that you would always be sick?
- Who told you that you would always be lonely?
- Who told you there was no hope?
- Who told you that God had no power?

I have come waving a banner. You're almost there. You can't quit. You can't give up. You may be weeping now, but joy does come in the morning.

# Self Assessment

What false information is the enemy feeding you?

_____

_____

_____

_____

_____

_____

List 5 New Daily Declarations that you will stand on:

_____

_____

_____

_____

_____

_____

_____

_____

# Who's Spotting You?

"Come to me, all you who are weary and burdened, and I will give you rest. Take my yoke upon you and learn from me, for I am gentle and humble in heart, and you will find rest for your souls. For my yoke is easy and my burden is light." St. Matthew 11:28-30

If there is an art to living, there must be an art to eating, cooking, shopping, saving and even exercising. When I started my exercise journey it was a true struggle. It wasn't until I changed my thinking and started viewing my exercise as a part of worship that it stopped feeling like a daily punishment. So now, almost a year later, I truly cherish the quiet time on my elliptical machine. For 60 minutes I close out the world and my worries, and it's just me and God.

While I may close out my worries and my mental to-do list, I am always aware of my surroundings. And every morning a group of six men come in to lift weights. Although they vary in size and age, they don't vary in stamina or ambition. Rain, sun or snow, they are there every morning to spot each other.

Spotting is simply the art of providing assistance to a person who is working out with weights. With a spotter, the lifter can push more than he could normally do alone. Correct spotting involves knowing when to assist with a lift and when to encourage the training partner to push beyond the point of pain. Spotting is a crucial component of resistance training because it exercises and enhances a lifter's mental and physical performance. Without the use of spotting, weight-lifting participants put themselves at a higher risk for injuries. The more I watch them, the more I have noticed that they never have anyone spotting them that they don't know. The more I study them in the morning, the more I realize that they don't have anyone spotting them that they don't trust.

The more I watch them, the more I realize that they never have anyone spotting them that can't lift their weight. In other words, a man lifting 300 pounds would also spot someone that can lift 300 pounds because if he gets in trouble or becomes fatigued, the spotter needs to be able to handle the weight. All I am trying to say is after everything that you have been through, why don't you trust God enough to give him your weight? Do you believe that God can handle those things in your life that are weighing you down? If you want to get through the rest of this year, and all the years to come, you're going to need to remind yourself that you have a "SPOTTER." He sees all and can handle the weight. You keep asking people to pray for you, but do you have a prayer life. You keep getting people to spot your problems, but they cannot solve their own.

I know this has been a tough year, but God wants to remind you He wasn't trying to crush you with the weight. He is pushing you beyond your comfort zone and building your endurance. He is pushing you beyond the comfort zone you've built around your prayer life. He's pushing you beyond the comfort zone you've built around your praise, and He's pushing you beyond the comfort zone you've built around studying His Word. Come out of that comfort zone, and build your muscles. He knows you could handle it because He is ready to spot you.

**Let us pray.**

*Gracious and merciful God, I thank you for this day. It's a day I've never seen before and will not see again. I come with a mouth full of praise and a heart of thanksgiving. I almost fainted, but I remembered that you are spotting me. Thank you God! The pressures of life almost stole my joy, but I remembered that you are spotting me. Thank you God! The news on the television almost broke my heart, but then I remembered that you are spotting me. Thank You God! Today I give you every care, concern and circumstance that is weighing me down! I decree and declare that the problems that I have faced this year have an expiration date. I decree and declare that the situation that's been keeping me up at night is going to be resolved before the New Year arrives. I decree and declare that before this month is over my territory will be enlarged.*

*God thank you for all that you have done in me, through me, and for me. Please don't stop until you finish what you have started in me. Don't allow me to leave this page the same way. In Jesus' name I pray. Amen.*

# I'm Finishing Strong!

"Therefore, since we are surrounded by such a huge crowd of witnesses to the life of faith, let us strip off every weight that slows us down, especially the sin that so easily trips us up. And let us run with endurance the race that God has set before us." Hebrews 12:1 NIV

My family and I joined about 400 colleagues, coworkers and friends at the retirement ceremony of my Aunt Deedee.

After walking five blocks in the rain, going through an extensive security check, and three different metal detectors, we were finally led into the Great Hall of the United States Department of Justice to celebrate her 39 years and 11 months of service to the Federal Government. During the two-hour ceremony we heard speech after speech about her winning personality, her relentless work ethic, her contagious faith, and her stellar leadership throughout the different stages of her career. She was presented with plaques, certificates, pictures, and all sorts of retirement memorabilia.

As the ceremony came to an end, I sat in my chair gazing at the long line of well-wishers that hugged my Auntie. I sat there looking at all of the photographers taking her pictures, and I thought about what she must have endured to get to that place. As I sat there, I thought about all of the challenges she must have faced as a Black woman. I thought about how many times she probably heard "no" before she got a "yes". I thought about how she had to handle her confidence being mislabeled as arrogance. I thought about all of the days she got there early or stayed late. I thought about the sacrifices she must have made and the lessons she had learned. I thought about all the days she must have gone to work when she didn't feel well.

And I thought, "From where did she get that unmovable audacity to think that she could go from the mailroom to the top the floor?" The questions started coming, and my mind started racing. When all of a sudden, God jumped in. "It's a decision." She made a cognitive analysis, a choice; she had an inner determination that she was going to finish strong.

If you really want to get through the rest of this year, you've got to do a cognitive analysis, and get some inner determination. Tell yourself "I am going to finish strong." Make up in your mind – no matter what you're going through or how it looks – "that he who began a good work in you will carry it on to completion until the day of Christ Jesus" (Philippians 1:6). You've got to make up in your mind that God is going to give you the power and strength to finish strong. You've got to make up in your mind today that the same energy, strategy, tenacity, prayer that it took you to start the New Year, God's going to give you in the days to come to finish strong. You've got to make up your mind today that you stand on the shoulders of a mighty cloud of witnesses, and you can finish strong.

My Auntie started in the mailroom, but she didn't finish in the mailroom. She started on the bus, but she didn't finish on the bus. She may have started out making $1.70 an hour, but she didn't finish there. You may have started this year bitter, but you've got to decide to finish it better. You may have started this day defeated, but you have to decide to finish it a winner. You may have started the day anxious, but you have to decide to finish it in peace.

Don't just stand there, get back out there. Catch your breath. Drink some water. Get a towel; wipe the sweat off of our face. Dry those tears. Dust off your shoulders. You're almost there!

**Let us pray.**

*Gracious and Merciful God, I come to you on this day, a day that I have never seen before and will never see again. I thank you for yesterday's portion, but I come seeking today's bread. I need a fresh blessing. I need a fresh miracle. I need fresh strength. I need a fresh revelation, so I can finish strong. I recognize that you are God and nothing is impossible for you. God, thank you for being a finisher. Please don't stop until you finish what you have started in me. In Jesus' name I pray. Amen*

# Don't Get Amnesia!

"Then Jesus said, "Did I not tell you that if you believe, you will see the glory of God?"  John 11: 40 NIV

I have been fascinated with law since I can remember.  I cherish my few Saturdays of nothingness when I can lay on my couch and watch marathons of Law and Order.  On one episode, the team was called to the hospital to investigate a robbery. A man had been attacked while walking his dog in Central Park.  During the attack the assailants took the victim's wallet, his identification, and ultimately his memory. When the investigators interviewed him, he couldn't remember his name or the incident.

If you really want to finish this year strong, remember what Jesus said.  We all get a little forgetful sometimes, but you've got to remember what Jesus said. There will be some days when all you have are the Lord's promises. Remember what Jesus said.  There will be some days when you don't want to praise, but remember what Jesus said.  There will be some days when you don't have strength, but remember what Jesus said.  There will be some days when you feel lonely, but remember what Jesus said.  In all your getting, remember what Jesus said.

He said,  "I will supply all of your needs according to my riches glory."  Not some of them or most of them, but all of your needs.

When you're insufficient, God promised that His grace would be sufficient. He promised that He would go before you. He promised that it would all work together for your good. Millions of people suffer from amnesia; don't be one of them. Don't lose your ability to recall the promises Jesus made to you. Learn them. Know them. Recall them. No matter where you are today or what you are going through, don't forget what Jesus said to you. God's promises don't change. They are still "yes" and "amen."

**Let us pray.**
*God, I come today like a dog chasing a bone. I am hungry and desperate for you.*

*I have chased after others things. I have chased after people, positions, titles, expectations, and I ran into a dead end. I have lived enough life, cried enough tears, and been through enough pain to know you are God. Seasons may change, people may change, times may change, but your love, your power, your grace, and your mercy are constant.*

*God it is in you that I live, move, breathe and have my being! Thank you for being amazing! Thank you being incredible! Thank you for being sovereign! Thank you for lifting up a standard against the enemies in my life! Amen.*

# You Will See It, Before I Share It!

"Meanwhile, the people were waiting for Zechariah and wondering why he stayed so long in the temple. When he came out, he could not speak to them. They realized he had seen a vision in the temple, for he kept making signs to them but remained unable to speak. When his time of service was completed, he returned home. After this his wife Elizabeth became pregnant and for five months remained in seclusion. The Lord has done this for me, she said. In these days he has shown his favor and taken away my disgrace among the people." Luke 1: 21-25 NIV

One of my favorite shows to watch during lunch is TLC's Baby Story. The show takes viewers on an intimate and emotional journey by profiling couples as they experience the final weeks of pregnancy and the first weeks of a new life. Viewers get an all-access-pass into the delivery room for a peek at the drama of labor and the unforgettable joy of the birth.

One of my favorite episodes was when a Vietnamese woman gave birth to a whopping 10-pound baby boy. He had the cutest chubby cheeks and the curliest black hair. What stood out to me, however, was what happened after mother and baby were released from the hospital. As they pulled up to their home in sunny California, she explained to reporters that in her culture mother and baby are confined to the home for the first 30 days of the newborn's life. They will not leave the house for anyone or anything unless it's a medical appointment. They do this because they are afraid of exposing the baby to anything his system is too young to fight off. After watching this story I couldn't help but think of Elizabeth. After being barren and disappointed for many years, she and Zechariah were finally expecting a baby. After all they had been through Elizabeth had every reason to be excited. After all the baby showers she had attended. After all the prayers she had prayed. After all the nights she had cried. It was finally her turn.

This was great news. It would have been understandable if Elizabeth had tweeted the good news, updated her Facebook status, sent out emails, or displayed her baby bump around town. The verse says the moment she found out she was expecting, she immediately isolated herself. She shut out the world and went into seclusion. Why? Because Elizabeth knew that she had to protect the integrity of her promise.

We don't know if she had morning sickness or strange cravings. All we know is she stayed in the house for five months. There's a lesson here. You've got to get into your mind, your spirit and your heart that everybody can't handle what you are about to deliver. Everybody can't handle your dream. Everybody can't handle your ambition. Everybody can't handle your wholeness. Everybody can't handle your prosperity. Everybody can't handle your deliverance. Everybody can't handle your anointing.

The Bible says, "For everything there is a season, a time for every activity under heaven. A time to be born and a time to die. A time to dance and time to weep. A time to laugh and a time to cry" (Ecclesiastes 3). That means there's a time to be public and a time to be private.

When you share what God is doing before it's time, you expose your "baby" to all types of toxins and attacks before the promise has actually been manifested. The Angel Gabriel had to tell Mary that her cousin Elizabeth was pregnant; Elizabeth hadn't even told her family the good news.

As we sit at the intersection of a New Year I have come to speak prophetically over your life. It does not yet appear the mighty and marvelous plans that God has specialized just for you. Just because you're not showing yet doesn't mean you're not expecting. God's word is not like our checks. It won't be returned back to you. Everything – and I do mean everything – God has promised you in private will be revealed in public. For now stop sharing it. God's going to show it in the New Year. Let them see it before you share it. **It's manifestation time.**

**Prayer:**
*Wow! Thank you God for the reminder. I will not abort or miscarry what you have deposited inside of me. There are six billion people on this earth, but you gave this gift to me. Thank you for trusting me to carry it. I don't take it lightly or for granted. My ear is to your mouth, and I promise that I won't share it until it's time for me to deliver. In Jesus' name I pray. Amen.*

# Hold On Help Is On The Way!

"As soon as they left the synagogue, they went with James and John to the home of Simon and Andrew. Simon's mother in law was in the bed with a fever, and they immediately told Jesus about her. So he went to her and took her hand and helped her up. The fever left her and she began to wait on them." - Mark 1: 29 – 39

I really believe all this modern technology is spoiling a generation of people. Microwaves, Text Messages, Twitter, Facebook, Emails. With the stroke of one button, you can cook a meal in a few minutes, with one stroke of one key, you can send an entire message across the world.

Because everything is so quick, effortless and convenient, we have evolved into a generation of people that is allergic to waiting.

We don't want to wait for anything or anybody.

We don't wait in line, traffic and ultimately we don't want to wait on God.

Which brings us to the heart of the matter. I know we keep hearing all of this "name it and claim it" theology. In all of my reading and study, I realized that God required something from all the recipients of His miracles...their participation.

You don't believe me, but I have threee witnesses. I want to call my first witness to the stand. The woman with the issue of blood. Which did she do? She had to touch the hem of Jesus' garment. Luke 8:(43-47)

Still not convinced. I want to call Witness Number 2 – The man with the withered hand. He had to stretch out his hand. Matthew 12 (9-14)

Witness Number 3- The Blind Man – Even after Jesus put spit and dirt on his eyes. He had to go down to the water and wash it off. John 9 (39 – 58)

So, I was baffled, when I ran into Peter's mother-in-law. It appeared to me that she didn't do anything. She didn't go anywhere. She didn't dial into any prayer calls. She didn't have to get up and meet Jesus. She didn't stand in any $100 offering lines. Yet, she still received her breakthrough. Yet, she still received her miracle.

And so, I scratched my head and reread the text. That's when I heard a little voice say, "she did do something." She waited. She had to hold on! She had to hold out! She had to wait until the Lord changed her condition! She had to wait with a fever in her body. She had to wait when the doctors were scratching their heads. She had to wait with doubt and fear lurking in the room. She had to wait with her back up against the wall.

She could have quit. She could have given up. She could have received the report of the doctor. She could have thrown in the towel. She could have started making final arrangements. She could have sunk into a depression. But she held on until Jesus got there.

I don't know what's given you a fever today. Maybe it's a fever in your body. Maybe it's a fever in your mind. Maybe it's a fever in your heart. Maybe it's a fever in your finances. Maybe it's a fever in your family. Maybe it's a fever on your job. Maybe it's a fever in your dreams.

I don't know how long you have had the fever, but God told me to tell you "HOLD ON! HELP IS ON THE WAY!" God has not forgotten about you. Your tears and prayers will not go unnoticed or unanswered. There is something that God is trying to teach you in the wait. There are some muscles God is trying to build and some fat God is trying to burn in the wait!

Whatever you do, if you have to use both hands and feet, "HOLD ON! HELP IS ON THE WAY!"

# A Few Rules for the Birthday Party!

"Then Herod called the Magi secretly and found out from them the exact time the star had appeared. He sent them to Bethlehem and said, Go and make a careful search for the child. As soon as you have found him, report to me, so that I too may go and worship him. After they had heard the king, they went on their way, and the star they had seen in the east went ahead of them until it stopped over the place where the child was. When they saw the star, they were overjoyed. On coming to the house, they saw the child with his mother Mary, and they bowed down and worshiped Him. Then they opened their treasures and presented Him with gifts of gold and of incense and of myrrh." Matthew 2:1-12 NIV

Birthday milestones are set along the paths of our lives to help reflect and celebrate who we are, where we have been, and ultimately where we are going. Whether it's a sweet 16, 30th, 50th, 60th, or even 70th birthday, we should reflect on God's creativity. While He was forming the moon, mountains, birds and the seas, He had us on his mind.

And, we get together year after year with our family and friends to celebrate the day of our birth. We have cake, balloons, flowers, and all types of gifts to help us celebrate our special day. But, I am realizing more and more that there is no birth as significant and meaningful as Jesus' birth. Jesus' birth was such a game changer that in the western hemisphere it literally split the time in half from BC to AD. Jesus' birth was such a game changer that when He was born, his mere presence tore the veil in the temple. In other words, there is no middle person between God and humanity. This is not just a regular birthday. Christmas is not just another day.

Christmas is a day when the world stops, businesses shut down, and Wall Street closes to celebrate the birth of the Lord of Lords and the King of Kings.

So in this holiday season, I just wanted to give you a few tips for enjoying those Christmas festivities. My first tip is don't forget the Birthday Boy. In all of your Christmas traditions, stories, activities, recipes, decorations, songs, gift exchanges, there cannot be a Christmas without Christ.

In all of your Christmas love and cheer, don't forget to reverence and love Jesus. The Bible says that as soon as the wise men saw Jesus, they immediately bowed down and worshipped him because they knew who He was. They knew what his birth meant not just to them, but for all of humankind.

Your worship says: "Nobody's birth has affected me like yours." Your worship says: "I don't want anything; I just want to lay at your feet." Your worship says: "I just want to thank you for being God." Your worship says: "I want to thank you for being sovereign and mighty." Your worship says, "You are the greatest gift."

My second tip is "don't be tardy for the party." Late is not the new norm. If Christmas dinner starts at 4 p.m. be there by 3:45. If

Christmas brunch starts at 10 a.m. be there by 9:45. As the wise men traveled to see Jesus they didn't make stops along the way. They arrived on time with gifts of gold, frankincense, and myrrh for the guest of honor.

My third tip is don't go to the party empty handed. In all your getting this Christmas, don't forget your manners. You may not have silver and gold, but my mother told me to never go anywhere empty handed. If you can't afford to make a dish offer to say the grace. If you can't afford to take a dessert volunteer to wash the dishes. If you can't afford to buy a gift show your loved ones some love with good deeds.

My fourth tip is be intentional in your gift-giving. Have you even thought about what you are going to give Jesus for his birthday? The fact is no outward gift can ever repay God for what He did for us. After all "He is the Wonderful Counselor, Mighty God, Everlasting Father, Prince of Peace" (Isaiah 9:6). What gifts can you give to honor the person who has given you eternal life? What gifts can you give to convey your love and appreciation to the one who is our EVERYTHING and has EVERYTHING?

Don't stress out. I have a few gift ideas:
- Give him the gift of your whole heart.
- Give him the gift of your whole mind.
- Give him the fruit of your lips.
- Give him your love.
- Give him your praise.
- Give him your service.
- Give him your adoration.

In the rush and fuss of Christmas parties, dinners, and social gatherings, make sure you don't forget about the guest of honor. Have fun catching up with family and friends, but be sure to make a joyful noise that will make heaven rejoice and hell frown. "Ain't no party like a Jesus party because a Jesus party don't stop!"

**Let us pray.**

*God it is in you that I live, move, breathe and have my being. I thank you for being Jehovah. Thank you for being my Jehovah Nissi - my Banner, Jehovah Rohi - my Shepherd, Jehovah Rapha- my Healer, Jehovah Shalom - my Peace, and Jehovah Jireh – my Provider. I thank you for revelation, confirmation and affirmation.*

*You are truly the best gift I have ever received. Just like you started in a manger and finished on the cross, please don't stop until you finish what you started in me. I ask that you give me traveling mercies as I travel to celebrate your birth with my loved ones. I ask that you arrest the spirit of excessive spending and holiday depression. I ask that you identify people, places and things that I can bless during the holidays.*

*Just like the wise men went another way home, I thank you for sending me new directions, new strategies, new tactics, new strength, new ideas, new favor, new mercy, new attitude, new habits, new relationships, new mentors, new joy, new peace, new provision and new finances for the New Year. You are great and still doing miracles. Happy Birthday Jesus! Amen.*

# Next Year I am Going a Different Way!

"After they had heard the king, they went on their way, and the star they had seen in the east went ahead of them until it stopped over the place where the child was. When they saw the star, they were overjoyed. On coming to the house, they saw the child with his mother Mary, and they bowed down and worshiped him. Then they opened their treasures and presented him with gifts of gold and of incense and of myrrh. And having been warned in a dream not to go back to Herod, they returned to their country by another route." Matthew 2 (9-12)

You would have to live under a rock to miss the anticipation in the atmosphere. We are at the intersection of parting ways with this year and crossing over into a new one. As the world prepares for parties, and saints prepare for worship I had to take inventory over my own life this year. What I realized is that you can't move forward until you embrace where you have been.

That led my thoughts to Watch Night services. What we celebrate today can be traced all the way back to the South on December 31, 1862, when they celebrated "Freedom's Eve." The Black community gathered in churches and homes all across the nation, anxiously awaiting news that the Emancipation Proclamation had actually become law. I don't know how they knew because there was no technology, but anticipation was in the air.

Historians say at the stroke of midnight, on January 1, 1863, all slaves in Confederate States were declared legally free by President Abraham Lincoln. When the news was received, there were prayers, shouts and songs of joy throughout the South. And history books say that our people fell to their knees and thanked God for making a way.

This blew my mind. The slaves had no money, no property, no adequate housing, but they had a praise. Their families had been separated and destroyed, but they had a praise. They had been treated like animals, but they had a praise. The women had been raped and the men had been beaten, but they still had a praise. You may not have five pennies to rub together to make a barn fire, but you should still have a praise.

You may not have a job, but you should still have a praise. You may not have a significant other, but you should still have a praise. You may not have all the answers for the coming year, but you should still have a praise!

It's Emancipation Time! "He who the Son sets free is free indeed" (John 8:36).

This year God has freed you from people, places and things, but the only way you are going to advance is to go a new way. There's nothing back there for you. After you finish giving God thanks, make up in your mind that you will move forward in the New Year. You won't turn around, but that you will go a different way.

Can you imagine a freed slave going back to the slave quarters to hang around? That's how silly you will look if you go back to people, places, habits, and thinking God has delivered you from.

Declare that your past is over and in God all things are made new. Surrender your life to Christ, and move forward.

Don't make a New Year's resolution. Make a Declaration. Say good-bye to last year. Farewell! So long! Arriverderci! Adios! Say hello to the New Year. It's time win, conquer, thrive, prosper, and rise. It's time to go another way!

**Let us pray!**
*God it is in you that I live, move, breathe and have my being. God when I look back over this year I know it was your hand that provided. When I almost threw in the towel, God your hand provided. When I almost lost my mind, God you brought peace to my mind. When I stood at the cemetery saying good bye to loved ones, you comforted me. When I was in the doctor's office getting that report, you provided. When I stood in the unemployment line, you provided. Thank you!*

*I thank you for being my Jehovah. Thank you for being my Jehovah Nissi - my Banner, Jehovah Rohi - my Shepherd, Jehovah Rapha- my Healer, Jehovah Shalom - my Peace, and Jehovah Jireh – my Provider. I thank you for revelation, confirmation and affirmation.*

*You are truly the best thing that ever happened to me! Please don't stop until you finish what you started in me. I am like Moses, I am not going into the New Year unless you go with me. Illuminate my strengths and identify my weaknesses! Just like the wise men went another way home, I thank you for allowing me to see a new year, new directions, new strategies, new tactics, new strength, new ideas, new favor, new mercy, new attitudes, new habits, new relationships, new mentors, new joy, new peace, new provision and new money, new babies, new marriages, new homes, and new businesses. You are great and still doing miracles!*

*"Now to him who is able to do immeasurably more than all we ask or imagine, according to his power that is at work within us,"* (Ephesians 3:20).

*In the undisputed, undefeated name of Jesus I pray. Amen.*

# About the Author

Akisha Sharon Greene is an entrepreneur, empowerment and small business coach, inspirational speaker, intercessor and conference host.

She is also the founder of First Friday's, a non-traditional, non-denominational monthly Bible study/ fellowship for women held on the first Friday of every month in Maryland.

First Friday's is not a clique or sorority. It is a movement, literally moving women from where they are to where God has called them to be in every area of life: physically, spiritually, financially, and socially.

Akisha has a bachelor's degree in sociology, certification in legal studies, and a master's degree in theology from Howard University.

She is biblically-based, socially sensitive, spiritually alive and radically in love with Jesus.

Akisha doesn't have an agenda! Her goals are simply to Empower, Encourage, and Equip the world, one WOMAN at a time.

*Join Us*

# FIRST FRIDAY'S

*Empowering, Equipping and
Encouraging the World,
One Woman at a Time!*

**www.firstfridaysfellowship.org**

202.399.3090